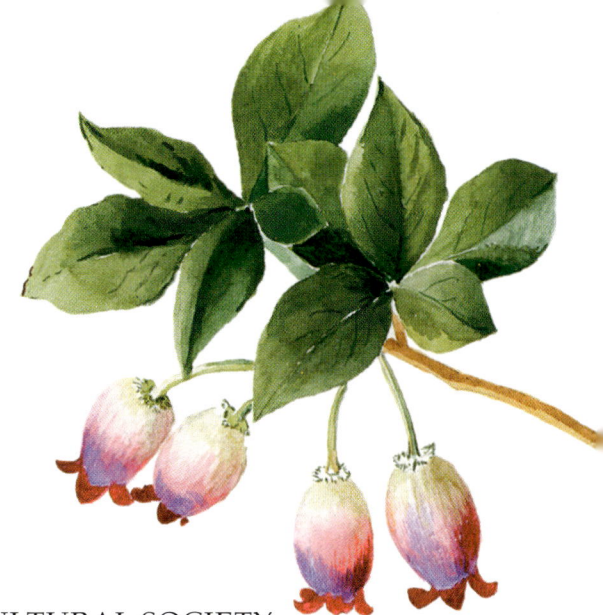

THE ROYAL HORTICULTURAL SOCIETY

DIARY 2010

Commentary by
Brent Elliott

Illustrations from
the Royal Horticultural Society's
Lindley Library

F

FRANCES LINCOLN LIMITED
PUBLISHERS

Frances Lincoln Limited
4 Torriano Mews
Torriano Avenue
London NW5 2RZ
www.franceslincoln.com

The Royal Horticultural Society Diary 2010
Copyright © Frances Lincoln limited 2009

Text and illustrations copyright © the Royal Horticultural Society 2009
and printed under licence granted by the Royal Horticultural Society, Registered Charity number 222879/SCO38262. For more information visit our website or call 0845 130 4646

An interest in gardening is all you need to enjoy being a member of the RHS.

Website: www.rhs.org.uk

First Frances Lincoln edition 2009

Astronomical information © Crown Copyright. Reproduced by permission of the Controller of Her Majesty's Stationery Office and the UK Hydrographic Office (www.ukho.gov.uk)

All rights reserved. No part of this publication may be reproduced, stored in a retrieval system or transmitted, in any form, or by any means, electronic, mechanical, photocopying, recording or otherwise, without either prior permission in writing from the publishers or a licence permitting restricted copying. In the United Kingdom such licences are issued by the Copyright Licensing Agency, Saffron House, 6–10 Kirby Street, London EC1N 8TS.

A catalogue record for this book is available from the British Library

ISBN: 978-0-7112-3000-2

Printed in China

1 2 3 4 5 6 7 8 9

RHS FLOWER SHOWS 2010

All shows feature a wide range of floral exhibits staged by the nursery trade, with associated competitions reflecting seasonal changes and horticultural sundries. With the exception of the shows held at Cardiff, Malvern, Chelsea, Hampton Court, Tatton Park and Wisley, all RHS Flower Shows will be held in one or both of the Society's Horticultural Halls in Greycoat Street and Vincent Square, Westminster, London SW1.

The dates given are correct at the time of going to press, but before travelling to a show, we strongly advise you to check with the Compass section of the RHS journal *The Garden*, or telephone the 24-hour Flower Show Information Line (020 7649 1885) for the latest details.

Front cover *Paeonia mascula* subsp. *russoi* 'Reverchoni'. Coloured drawing, dated 1934, by Lilian Snelling, for a plate in Sir Frederick Stern's *Study of the genus Paeonia* (1946).

Back cover *Linaria vulgaris*. Coloured drawing, undated, by Lilian Snelling.

Title page *Menziesia ciliicalyx*. Coloured drawing, undated, by Lilian Snelling, probably made for H.J. Elwes.

Overleaf, left *Paeonia whittmanniana* [sic = *wittmanniana*] var. *nudicarpa*. Coloured drawing by Lilian Snelling, made in May 1931.

CALENDAR 2010

JANUARY
M	T	W	T	F	S	S
				1	2	3
4	5	6	7	8	9	10
11	12	13	14	15	16	17
18	19	20	21	22	23	24
25	26	27	28	29	30	31

FEBRUARY
M	T	W	T	F	S	S
1	2	3	4	5	6	7
8	9	10	11	12	13	14
15	16	17	18	19	20	21
22	23	24	25	26	27	28

MARCH
M	T	W	T	F	S	S
1	2	3	4	5	6	7
8	9	10	11	12	13	14
15	16	17	18	19	20	21
22	23	24	25	26	27	28
29	30	31				

APRIL
M	T	W	T	F	S	S
			1	2	3	4
5	6	7	8	9	10	11
12	13	14	15	16	17	18
19	20	21	22	23	24	25
26	27	28	29	30		

MAY
M	T	W	T	F	S	S
					1	2
3	4	5	6	7	8	9
10	11	12	13	14	15	16
17	18	19	20	21	22	23
24	25	26	27	28	29	30
31						

JUNE
M	T	W	T	F	S	S
	1	2	3	4	5	6
7	8	9	10	11	12	13
14	15	16	17	18	19	20
21	22	23	24	25	26	27
28	29	30				

JULY
M	T	W	T	F	S	S
			1	2	3	4
5	6	7	8	9	10	11
12	13	14	15	16	17	18
19	20	21	22	23	24	25
26	27	28	29	30	31	

AUGUST
M	T	W	T	F	S	S
						1
2	3	4	5	6	7	8
9	10	11	12	13	14	15
16	17	18	19	20	21	22
23	24	25	26	27	28	29
30	31					

SEPTEMBER
M	T	W	T	F	S	S
		1	2	3	4	5
6	7	8	9	10	11	12
13	14	15	16	17	18	19
20	21	22	23	24	25	26
27	28	29	30			

OCTOBER
M	T	W	T	F	S	S
				1	2	3
4	5	6	7	8	9	10
11	12	13	14	15	16	17
18	19	20	21	22	23	24
25	26	27	28	29	30	31

NOVEMBER
M	T	W	T	F	S	S
1	2	3	4	5	6	7
8	9	10	11	12	13	14
15	16	17	18	19	20	21
22	23	24	25	26	27	28
29	30					

DECEMBER
M	T	W	T	F	S	S
		1	2	3	4	5
6	7	8	9	10	11	12
13	14	15	16	17	18	19
20	21	22	23	24	25	26
27	28	29	30	31		

CALENDAR 2011

JANUARY
M	T	W	T	F	S	S
					1	2
3	4	5	6	7	8	9
10	11	12	13	14	15	16
17	18	19	20	21	22	23
24	25	26	27	28	29	30
31						

FEBRUARY
M	T	W	T	F	S	S
	1	2	3	4	5	6
7	8	9	10	11	12	13
14	15	16	17	18	19	20
21	22	23	24	25	26	27
28						

MARCH
M	T	W	T	F	S	S
	1	2	3	4	5	6
7	8	9	10	11	12	13
14	15	16	17	18	19	20
21	22	23	24	25	26	27
28	29	30	31			

APRIL
M	T	W	T	F	S	S
				1	2	3
4	5	6	7	8	9	10
11	12	13	14	15	16	17
18	19	20	21	22	23	24
25	26	27	28	29	30	

MAY
M	T	W	T	F	S	S
						1
2	3	4	5	6	7	8
9	10	11	12	13	14	15
16	17	18	19	20	21	22
23	24	25	26	27	28	29
30	31					

JUNE
M	T	W	T	F	S	S
		1	2	3	4	5
6	7	8	9	10	11	12
13	14	15	16	17	18	19
20	21	22	23	24	25	26
27	28	29	30			

JULY
M	T	W	T	F	S	S
				1	2	3
4	5	6	7	8	9	10
11	12	13	14	15	16	17
18	19	20	21	22	23	24
25	26	27	28	29	30	31

AUGUST
M	T	W	T	F	S	S
1	2	3	4	5	6	7
8	9	10	11	12	13	14
15	16	17	18	19	20	21
22	23	24	25	26	27	28
29	30	31				

SEPTEMBER
M	T	W	T	F	S	S
			1	2	3	4
5	6	7	8	9	10	11
12	13	14	15	16	17	18
19	20	21	22	23	24	25
26	27	28	29	30		

OCTOBER
M	T	W	T	F	S	S
					1	2
3	4	5	6	7	8	9
10	11	12	13	14	15	16
17	18	19	20	21	22	23
24	25	26	27	28	29	30
31						

NOVEMBER
M	T	W	T	F	S	S
	1	2	3	4	5	6
7	8	9	10	11	12	13
14	15	16	17	18	19	20
21	22	23	24	25	26	27
28	29	30				

DECEMBER
M	T	W	T	F	S	S
			1	2	3	4
5	6	7	8	9	10	11
12	13	14	15	16	17	18
19	20	21	22	23	24	25
26	27	28	29	30	31	

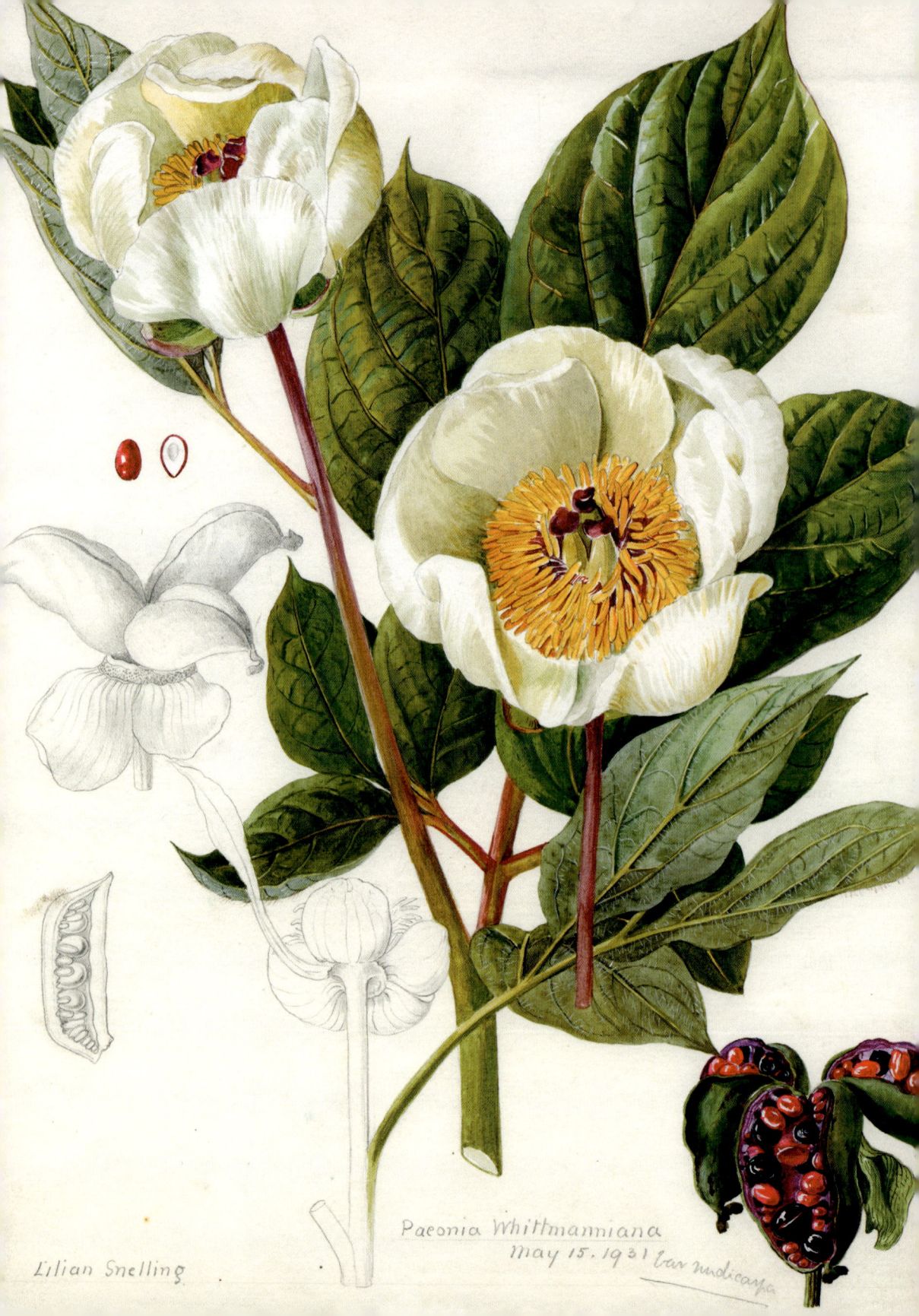

LILIAN SNELLING 1879–1972

"Her work as a botanical artist is without living peer [and] as a botanical illustrator and technician her work materially eclipses that of Redoute," wrote the distinguished botanist Dr George Lawrence, on hearing of the death of Lilian Snelling.

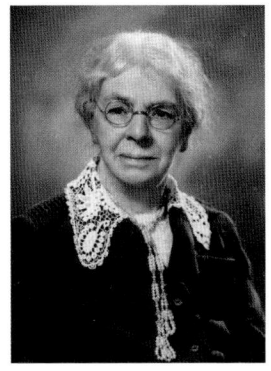

Lilian Snelling was born in St Mary Cray in Kent to a well-known family of millers. The youngest of the family, she spent most of her life in St Mary Cray, living with her three other unmarried sisters in Spring Hall, the family home. The illustrations in this volume represent examples of her work throughout her career. The examples of her earliest surviving work were painted in the fields and hedgerows of Kent around St Mary Cray and nearby Tunbridge Wells. These composite pictures, which formed the sketchbook she kept in her early twenties, were completed over a period of time.

After studying art and lithography at the Royal College of Art in London, she worked as the protégée of the arboriculturalist and plant hunter Henry John Elwes (1846–1922), painting plants that grew in his garden at Colesbourne in Gloucestershire. Many of these images are included in this diary. (When Arthur Grove published two supplements to Elwes' *Monograph of the Genus Lilium*, 1933–40, it was to Lilian Snelling that he turned for the magnificent illustrations, which are regarded as her masterpiece.)

From 1916 to 1921 Lilian Snelling worked at the Royal Botanic Garden, Edinburgh, under the guidance of the Keeper, Sir Isaac Bayley Balfour, and it was there that she developed the meticulous style that was to stand her in such good stead on *Curtis's Botanical Magazine*, which had been purchased by the Royal Horticultural Society in 1921.

In 1922 she was hired as the magazine's principal illustrator and lithographer and, over a period of thirty years, she made over 740 plates, an achievement that put her at the forefront of her art. Volume 169 was dedicated to her, with praise for her "remarkable delicacy of accurate outlines, brilliancy of colour and intricate gradation of tone".

Lilian Snelling retired from the *Botanical Magazine* in 1952. She was awarded the MBE in 1954 and the Victoria Medal of Honour, the Royal Horticultural Society's highest award, in 1955. The last of the sisters to survive, she died at the age of ninety-three.

The flowering of Lilian Snelling's mature style formed the outstanding model for British botanical artists since then. The illustrations in this diary represent examples from all periods of her long career.

Brent Elliott

THE ROYAL HORTICULTURAL SOCIETY

DECEMBER & JANUARY

WEEK **1**

28 *Monday* — Holiday, UK

29 *Tuesday*

30 *Wednesday*

31 *Thursday* — New Year's Eve
Full Moon

1 *Friday* — New Year's Day
Holiday, UK, Republic of Ireland, Canada,
USA, Australia and New Zealand

2 *Saturday* — Holiday, Scotland

3 *Sunday*

Dendrobium Thwaitesiae. Coloured drawing, dated April 1915,
by Lilian Snelling, probably made for H.J. Elwes.

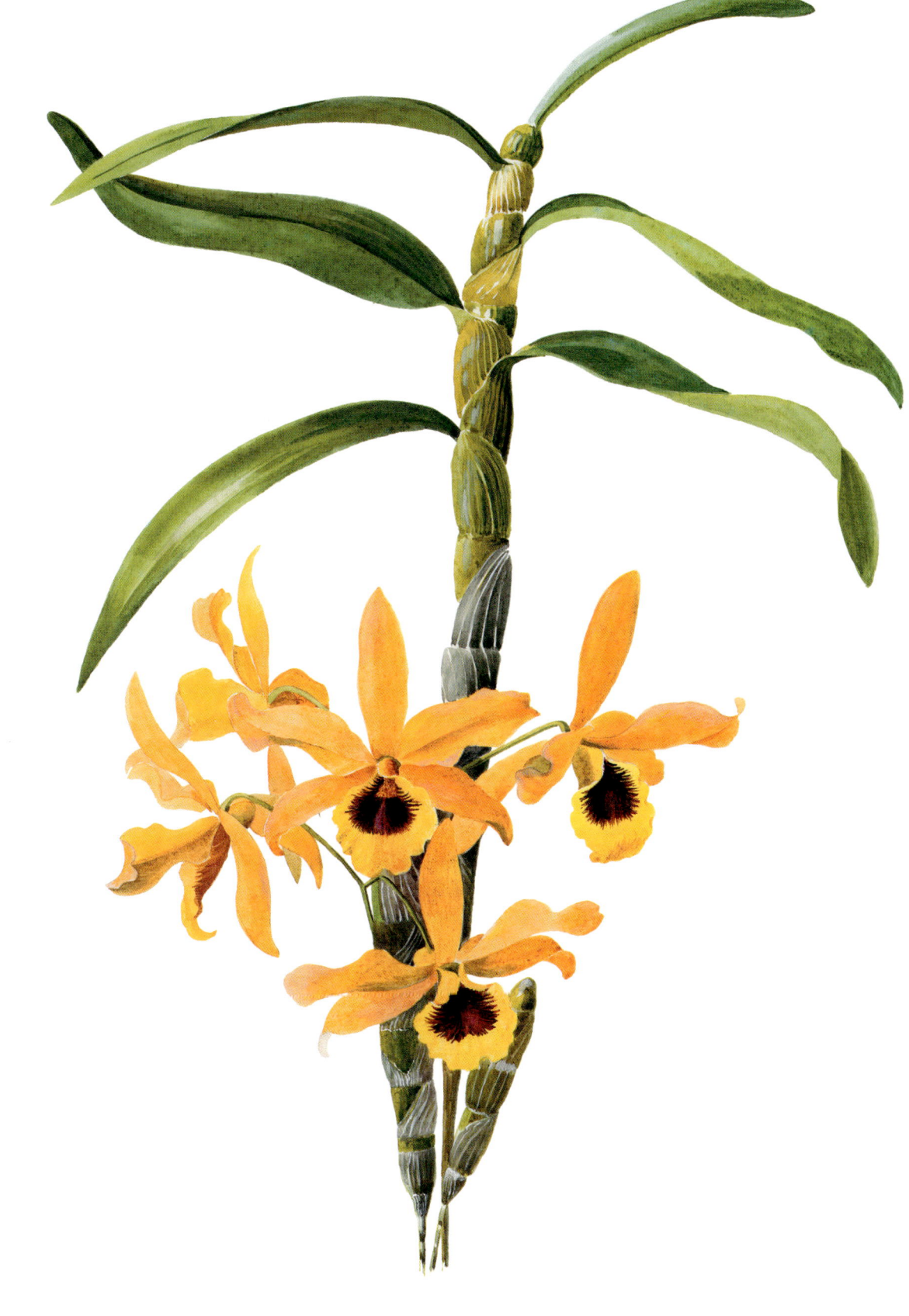

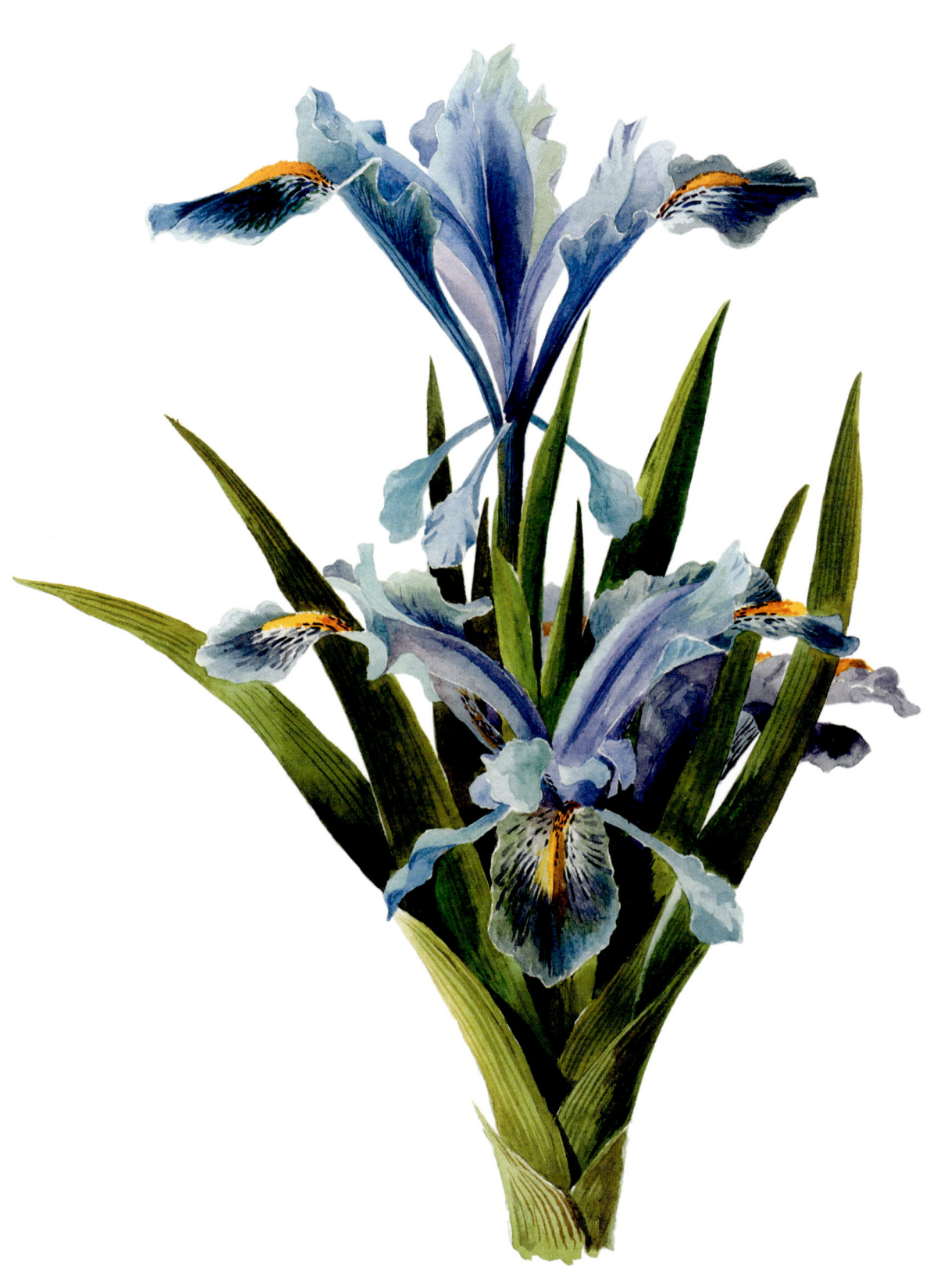

WEEK **2**

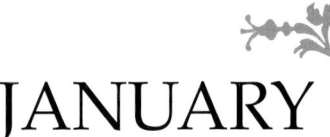

JANUARY

Holiday, Scotland (subject to confirmation)
Holiday, New Zealand

Monday **4**

Tuesday **5**

Epiphany

Wednesday **6**

Last Quarter

Thursday **7**

Friday **8**

Saturday **9**

Sunday **10**

Iris xiphium 'Pur-sind' (a hybrid bred by the Dutch nursery house of Van Tubergen, a cross between *Iris persica* 'Purpurea' and *Iris sindjarensis* [now *Iris aucheri*]). Coloured drawing by Lilian Snelling, made for H.J. Elwes of Colesbourne in March 1915.

JANUARY

WEEK 3

11 *Monday*

12 *Tuesday*

13 *Wednesday*

14 *Thursday*

15 *Friday* — *New Moon*

16 *Saturday*

17 *Sunday*

Coelogyne corymbosa. Coloured drawing by Lilian Snelling, made in March 1915 for H.J. Elwes of Colesbourne, who had collected the plant in Sikkim the previous year.

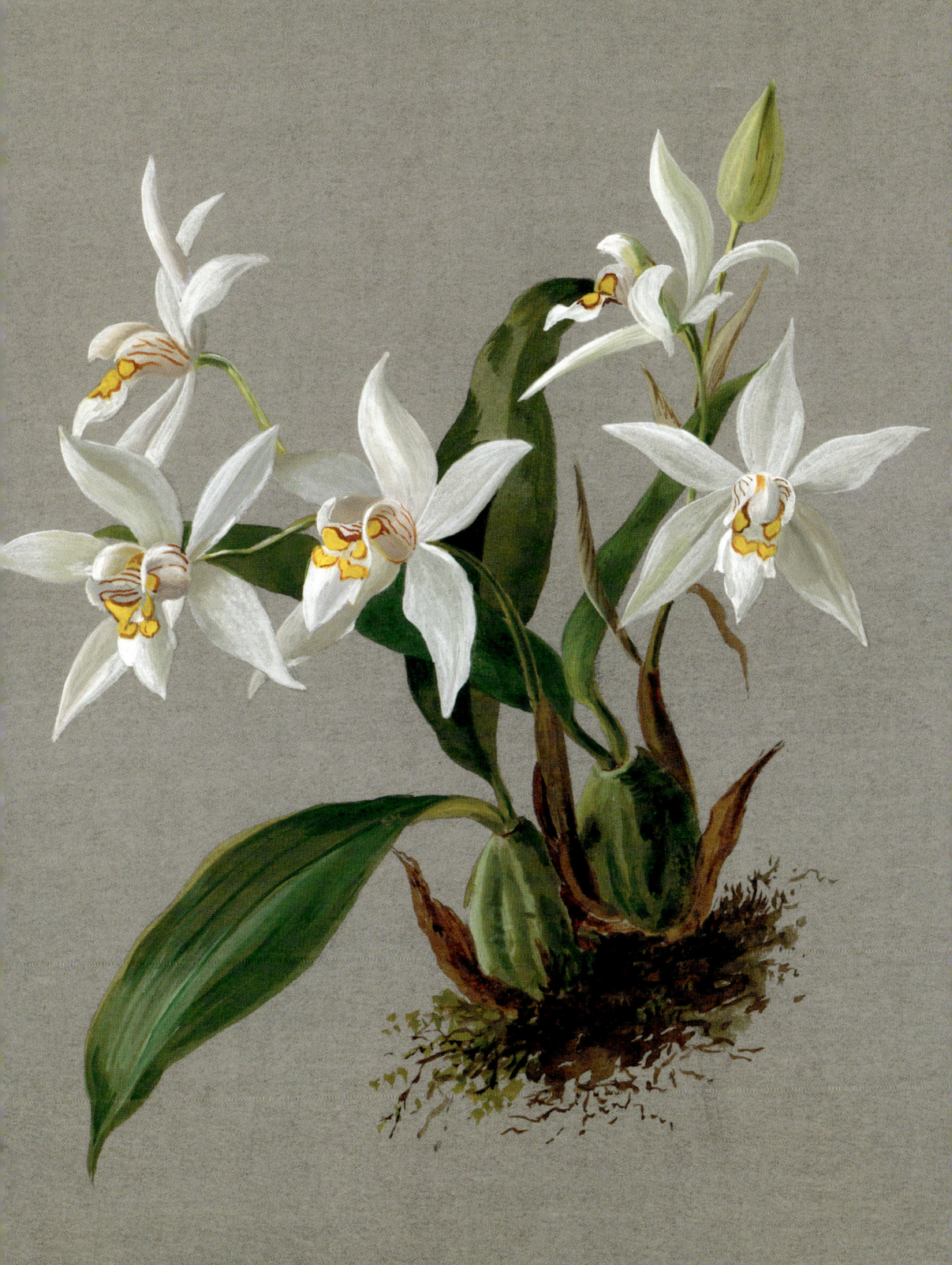

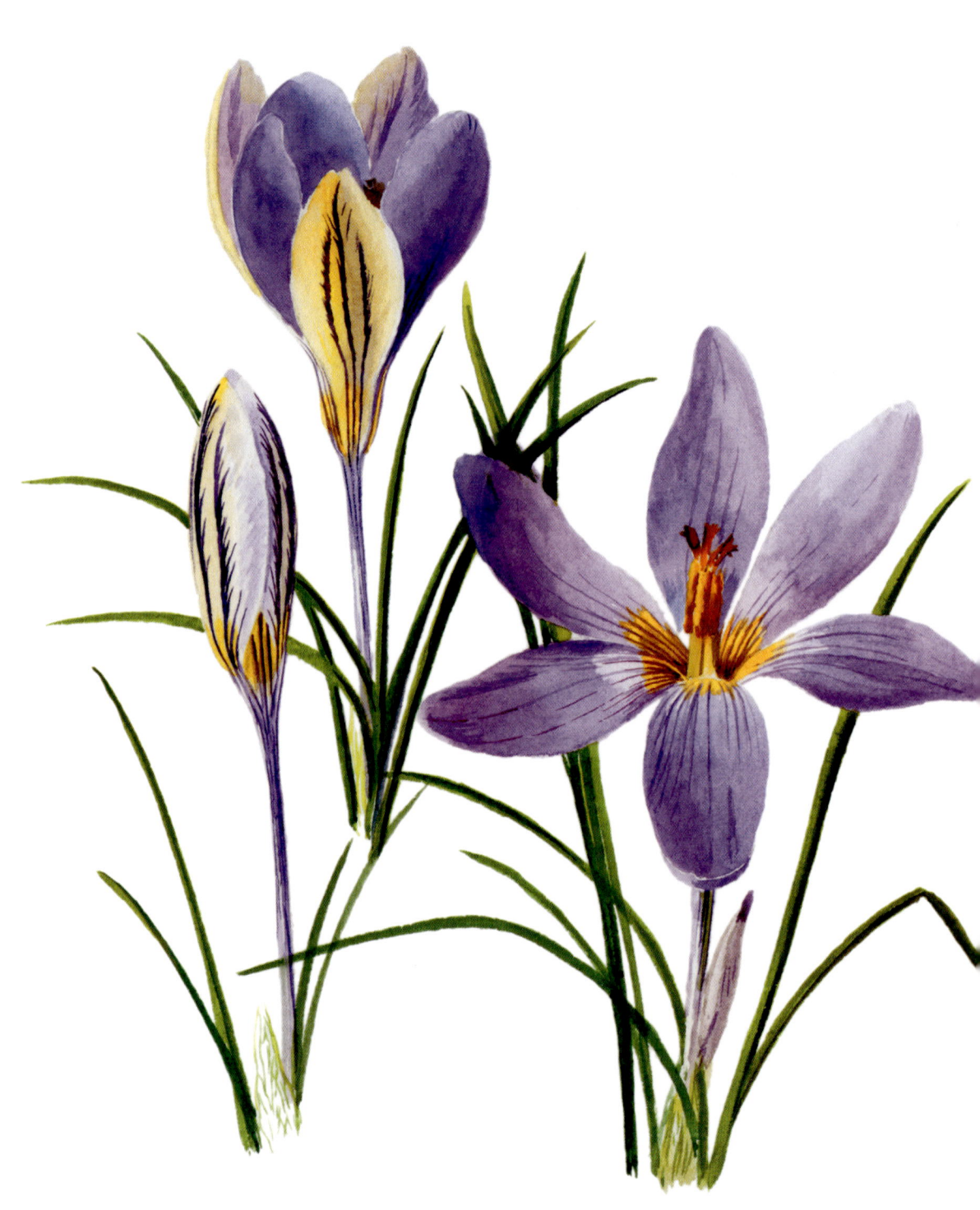

WEEK **4**

JANUARY

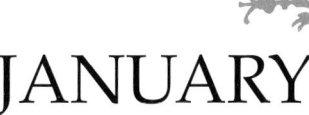

Holiday, USA (Martin Luther King's Birthday)   *Monday* **18**

Tuesday **19**

Wednesday **20**

Thursday **21**

Friday **22**

First Quarter   *Saturday* **23**

Sunday **24**

Crocus imperati and *Crocus sieberi* subsp. *atticus*.
Coloured drawing by Lilian Snelling, made for
H.J. Elwes of Colesbourne in February 1915.

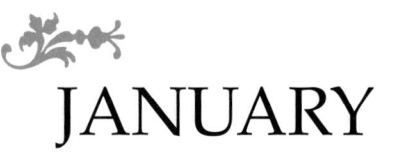

JANUARY

WEEK 5

25 *Monday*

26 *Tuesday* Holiday, Australia (Australia Day)

27 *Wednesday*

28 *Thursday*

29 *Friday*

30 *Saturday* *Full Moon*

31 *Sunday*

Camellia sasanqua. Coloured drawing, dated November 1915, by Lilian Snelling, made at the Cambridge Botanic Garden.

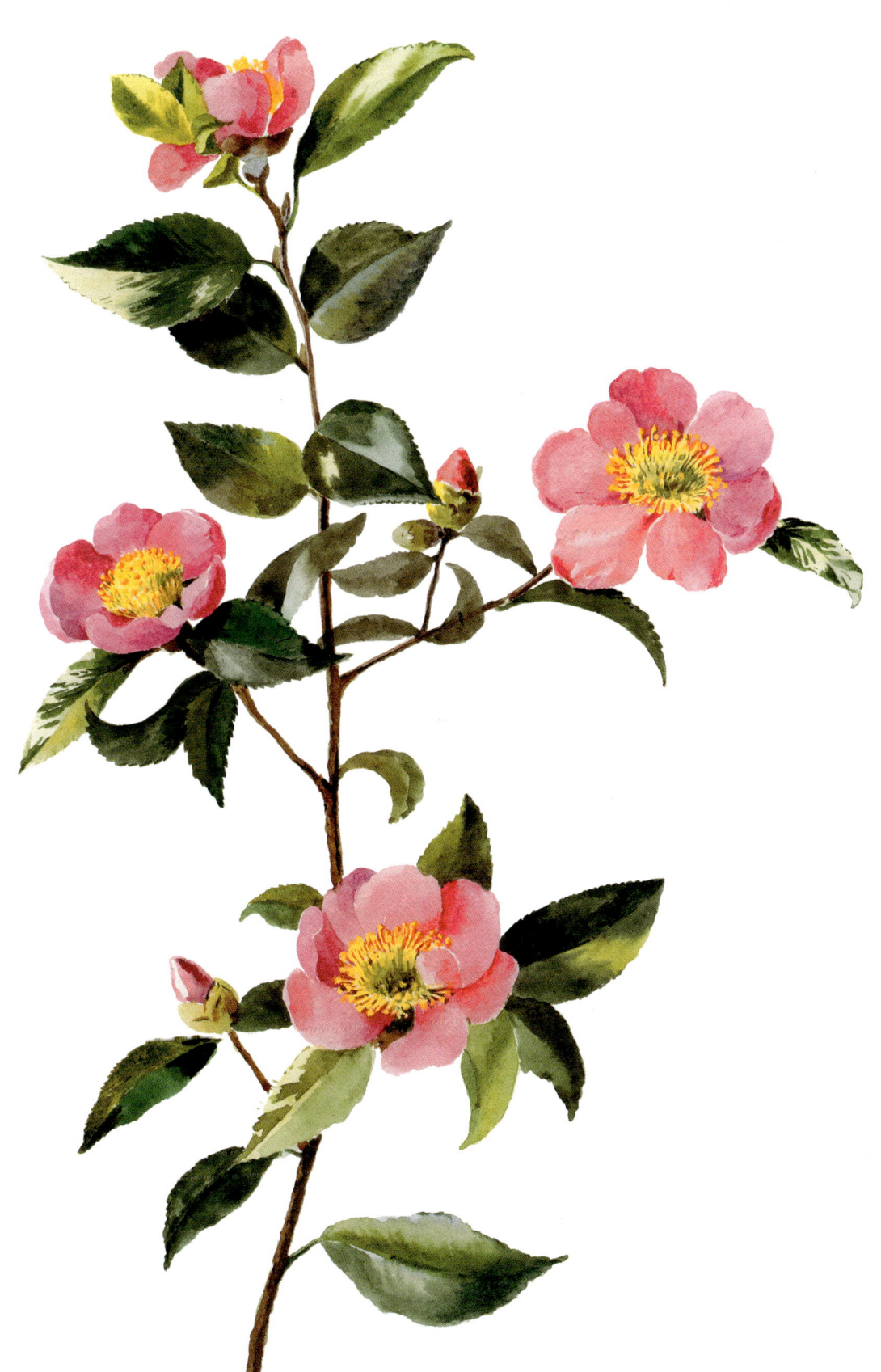

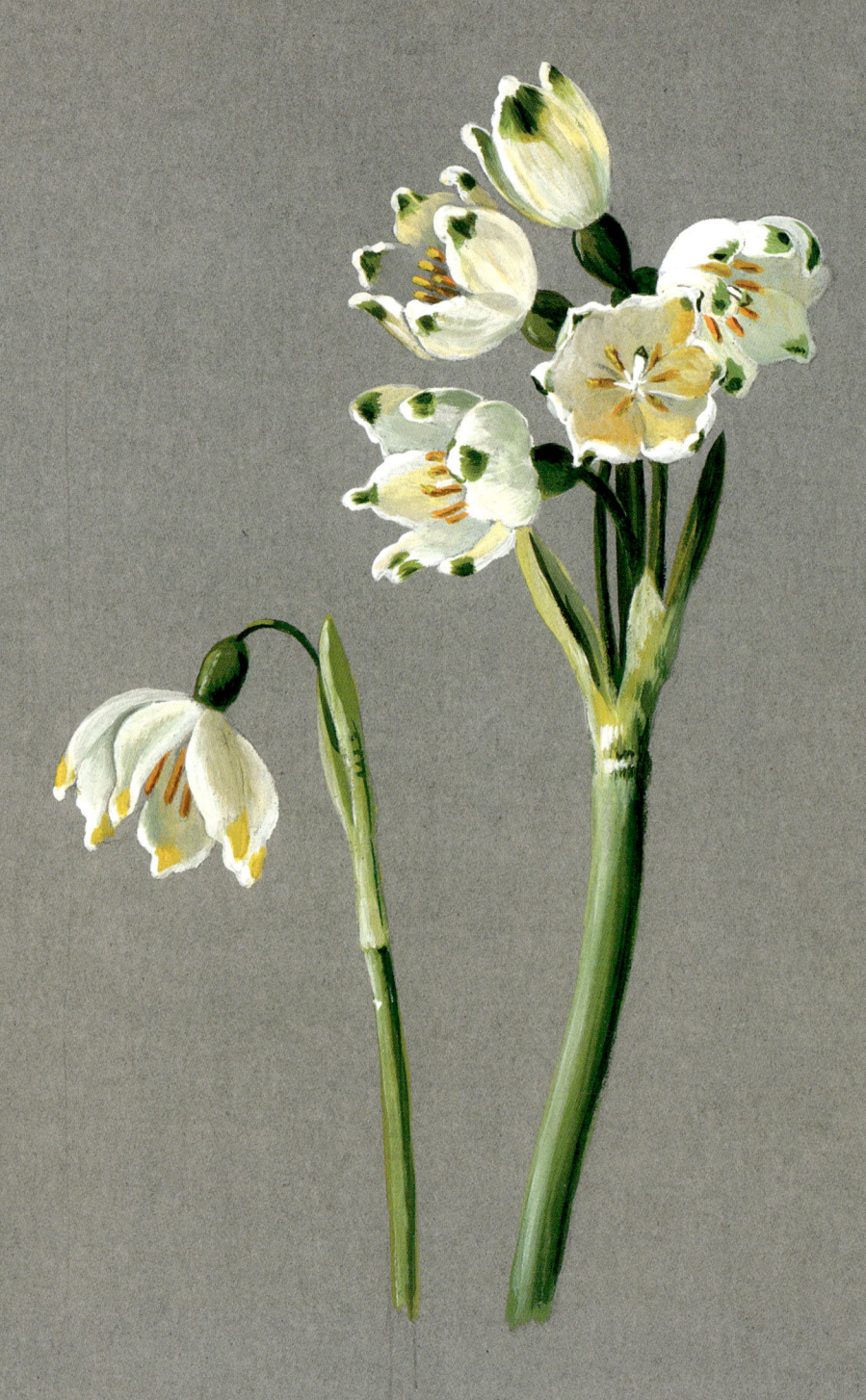

WEEK **6**

FEBRUARY

Monday **1**

Tuesday **2**

Wednesday **3**

Thursday **4**

Last Quarter

Friday **5**

Accession of Queen Elizabeth II
Holiday, New Zealand (Waitangi Day)

Saturday **6**

Sunday **7**

Leucojum vernum var. *carpathicum* 'Multiflora'.
Coloured drawing by Lilian Snelling, made for
H.J. Elwes of Colesbourne in February 1916.

FEBRUARY

WEEK **7**

8 *Monday*

9 *Tuesday*

10 *Wednesday*

11 *Thursday*

12 *Friday*

13 *Saturday*

14 *Sunday*

St. Valentine's Day
Chinese New Year
New Moon

Primula vulgaris, Hyacinthoides non-scripta, Primula veris, Parietaria judaica: an early coloured drawing by Lilian Snelling of plants around her family home at St Mary Cray, made from May to August 1901.

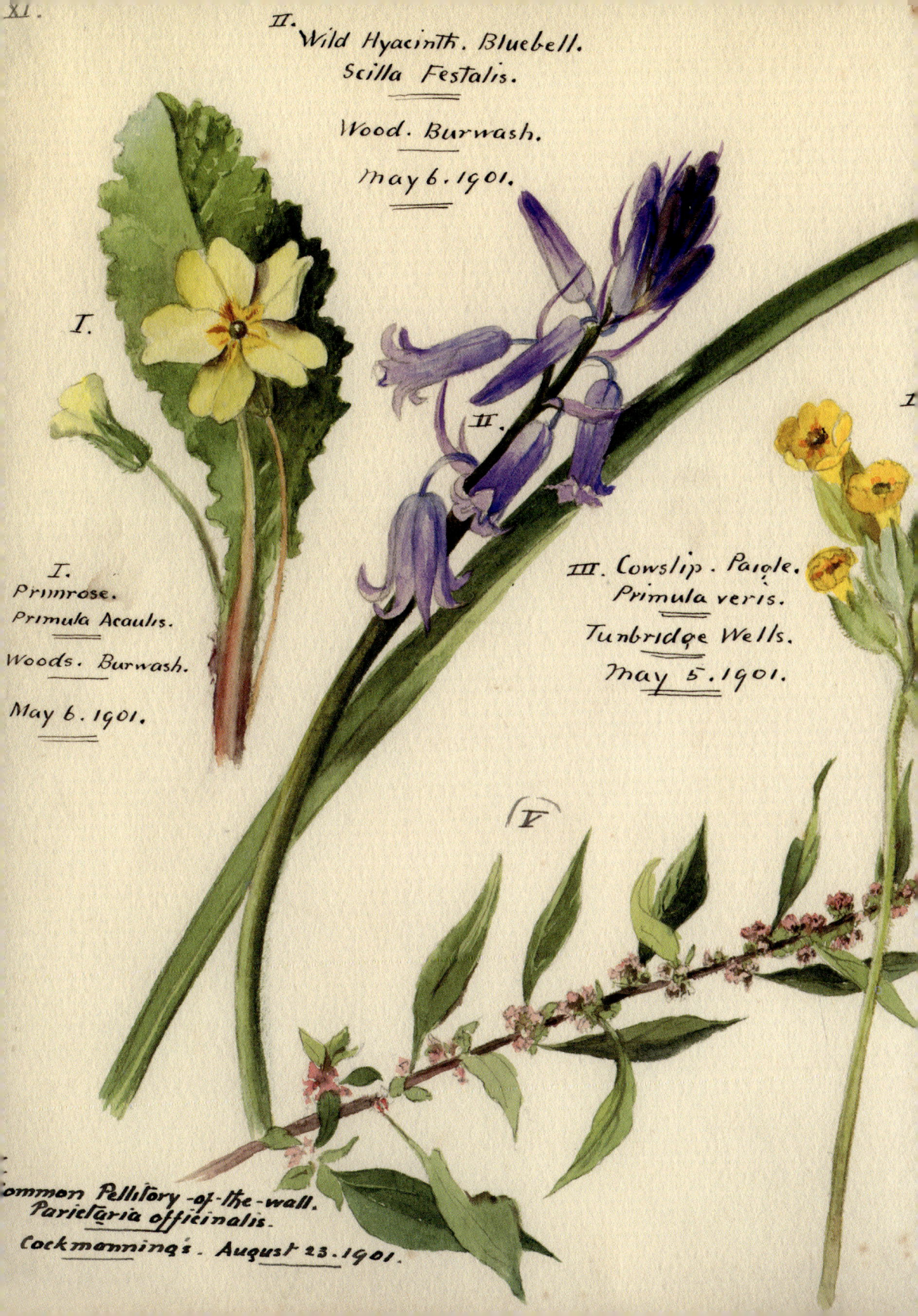

II. Wild Hyacinth. Bluebell.
Scilla Festalis.
Wood. Burwash.
May 6. 1901.

I. Primrose.
Primula Acaulis.
Woods. Burwash.
May 6. 1901.

III. Cowslip. Paigle.
Primula veris.
Tunbridge Wells.
May 5. 1901.

Common Pellitory-of-the-wall.
Parietaria officinalis.
Cockmannings. August 23. 1901.

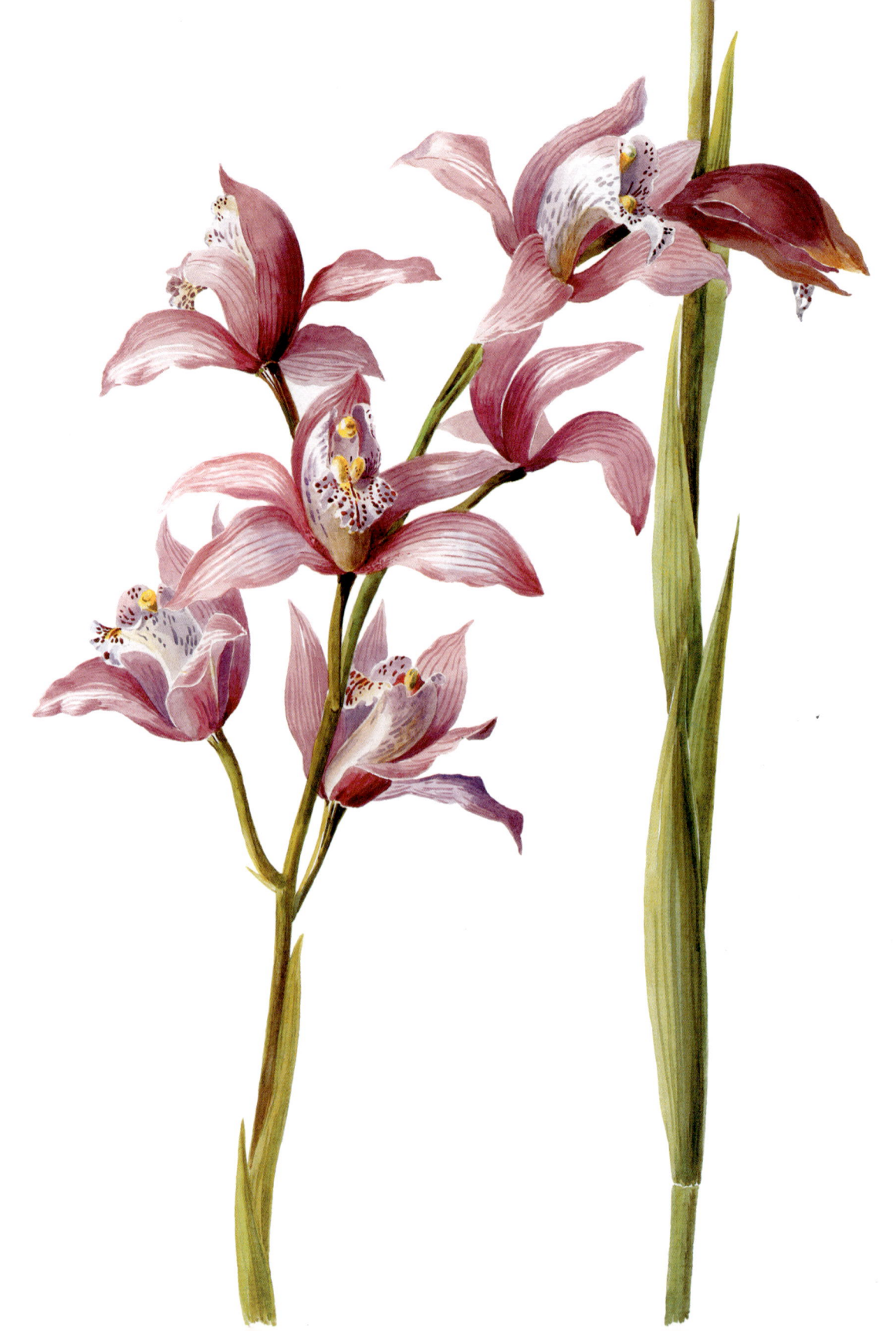

WEEK **8**

FEBRUARY

Holiday, USA (Washington's Birthday)   *Monday* **15**

Shrove Tuesday   *Tuesday* **16**
RHS London Plant and Design Show

Ash Wednesday   *Wednesday* **17**
RHS London Plant and Design Show

Thursday **18**

Friday **19**

Saturday **20**

Sunday **21**

Cymbidium Alexanderi. Coloured drawing by Lilian Snelling, made for H.J. Elwes of Colesbourne in 1915.

FEBRUARY

WEEK **9**

22 *Monday* — *First Quarter*

23 *Tuesday*

24 *Wednesday*

25 *Thursday*

26 *Friday*

27 *Saturday*

28 *Sunday* — *Full Moon*

Narcissus pseudonarcissus. Coloured drawing, undated, by Lilian Snelling.

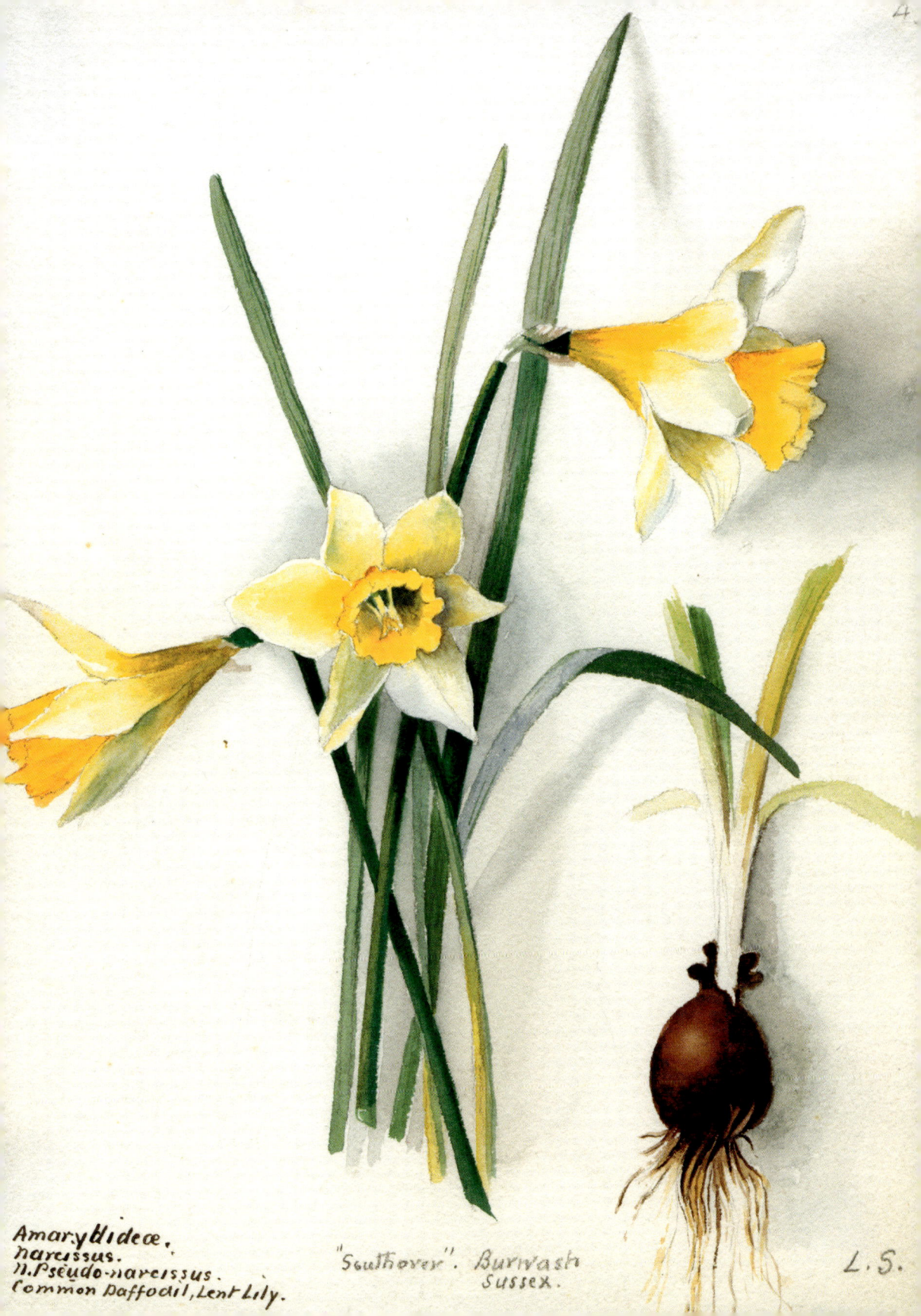

Amaryllideæ.
Narcissus.
N. Pseudo-narcissus.
Common Daffodil, Lent Lily.

"Southover". Burwash
Sussex.

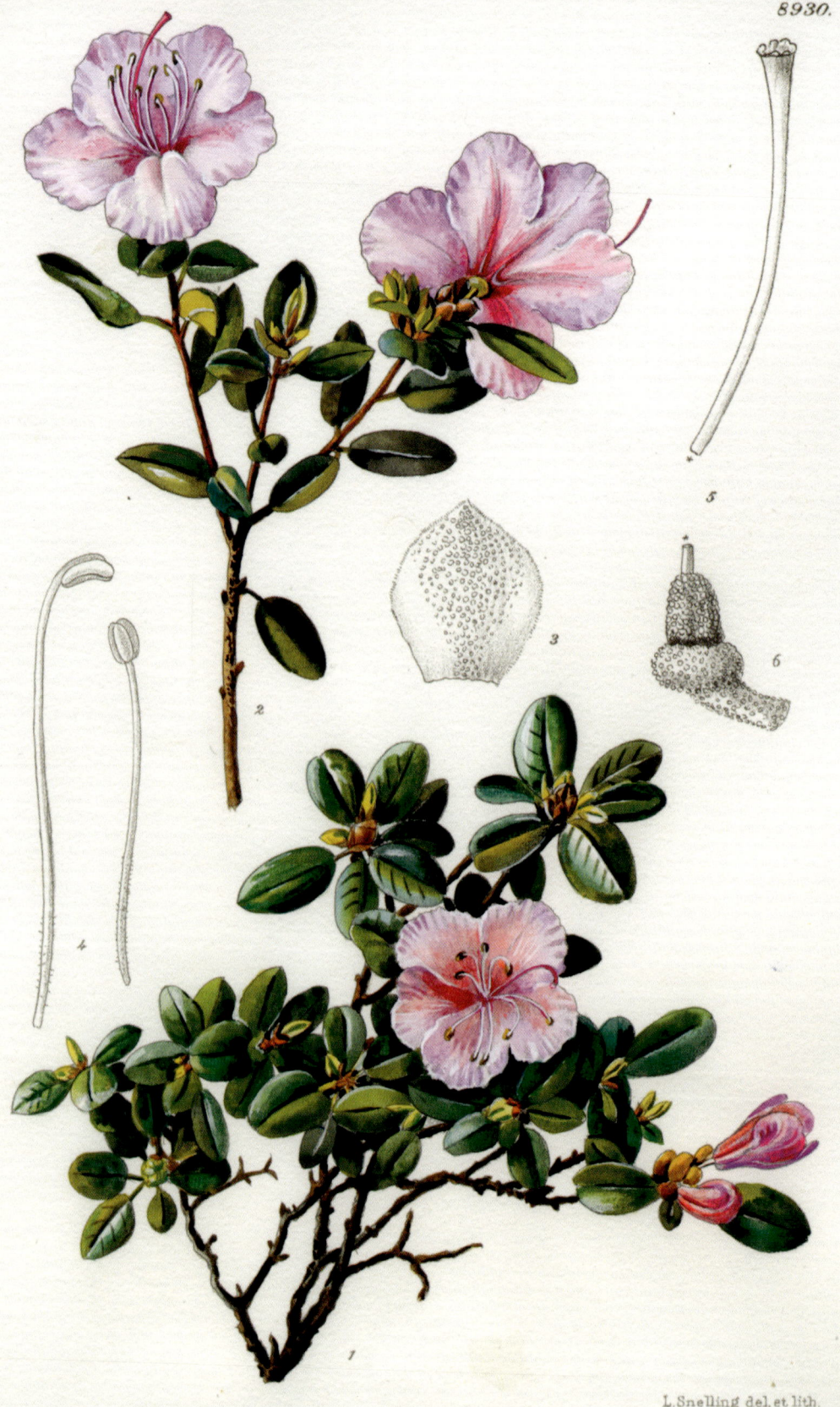

WEEK **10**

MARCH

St. David's Day

Monday **1**

Tuesday **2**

Wednesday **3**

Thursday **4**

Friday **5**

Saturday **6**

Last Quarter

Sunday **7**

Rhododendron dauricum 'Sempervirens'. Hand-coloured proof plate by Lilian Snelling, for plate 8930 of *Curtis's Botanical Magazine* (1938).

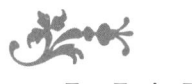

MARCH

WEEK **11**

8 *Monday*
Commonwealth Day
Holiday, Australia (Canberra Day)

9 *Tuesday*

10 *Wednesday*

11 *Thursday*

12 *Friday*

13 *Saturday*

14 *Sunday*
Mothering Sunday, UK

Primula × anisodoxa. Coloured drawing, dated May 1916, by Lilian Snelling, made at the Edinburgh Botanic Garden.

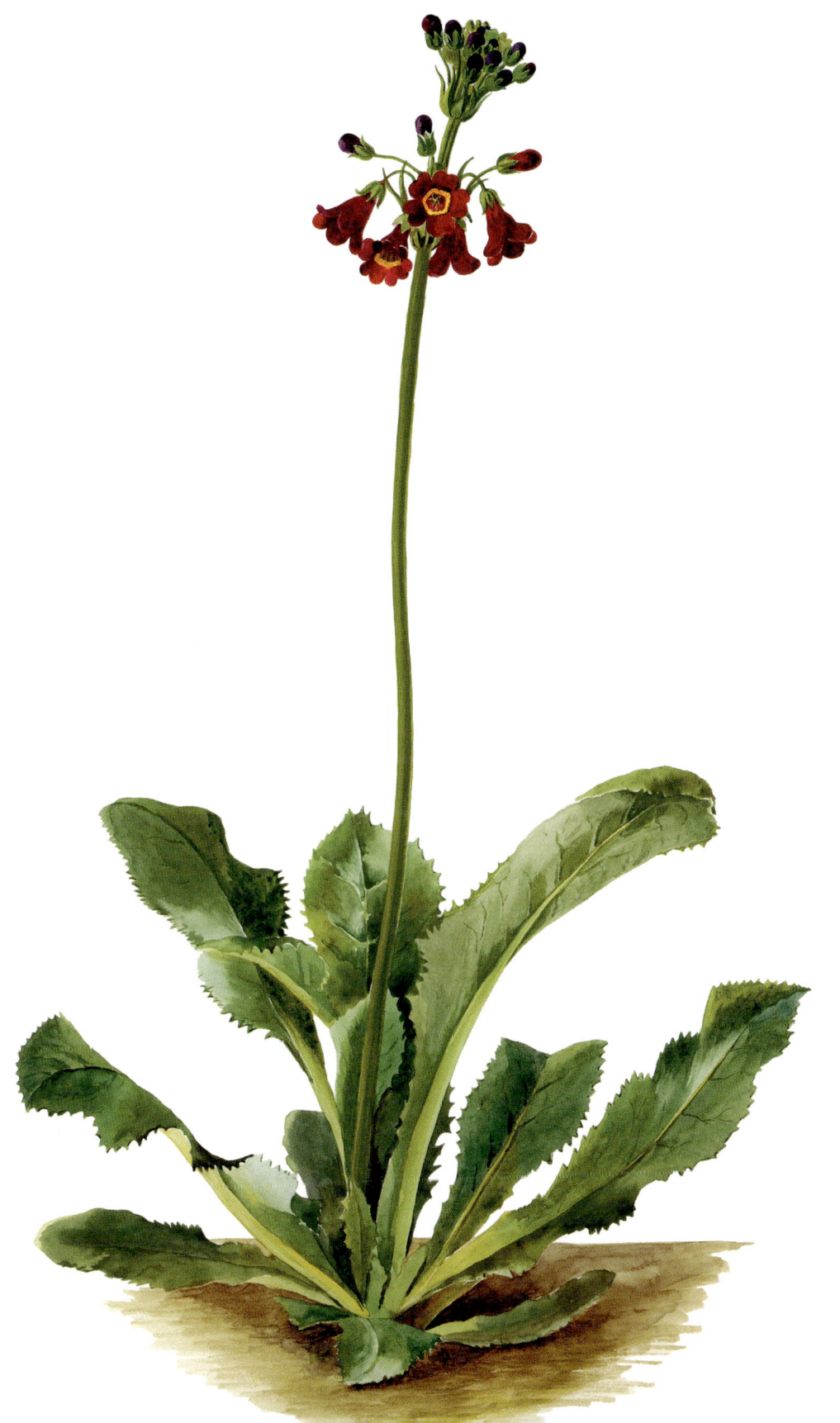

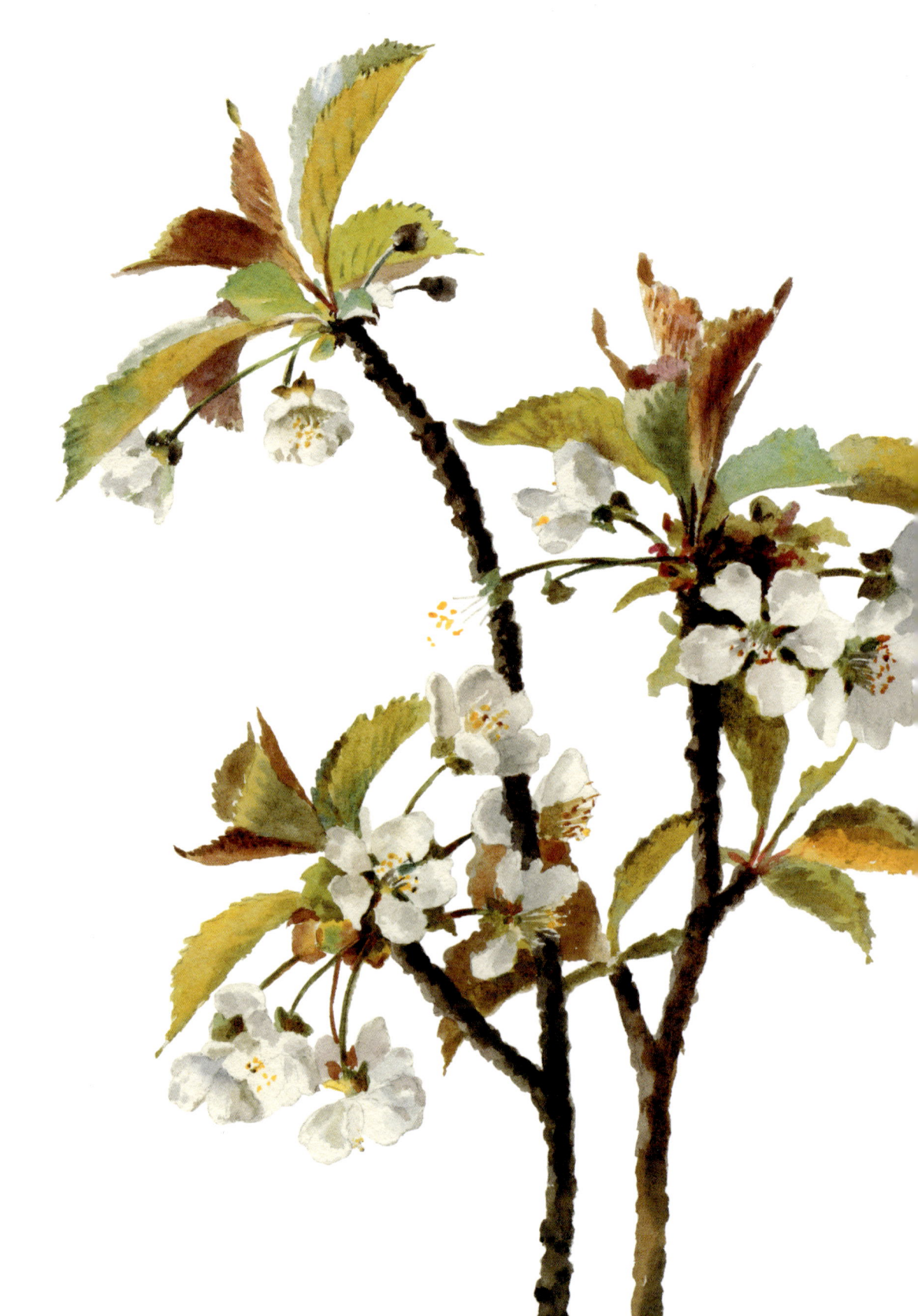

WEEK **12**

MARCH

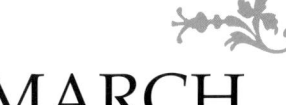

Monday **15**

Tuesday **16**

St. Patrick's Day
Holiday, Northern Ireland and Republic of Ireland

Wednesday **17**

Thursday **18**

Friday **19**

Vernal Equinox (Spring begins)
RHS London Orchid Show

Saturday **20**

RHS London Orchid Show

Sunday **21**

Prunus avium. Coloured drawing, undated, by Lilian Snelling.

MARCH

WEEK **13**

22 *Monday*

23 *Tuesday*   *First Quarter*

24 *Wednesday*

25 *Thursday*

26 *Friday*

27 *Saturday*

28 *Sunday*   British Summer Time begins
Palm Sunday

Tulipa fosteriana. Coloured drawing by Lilian Snelling, made for H.J. Elwes of Colesbourne in April 1905.

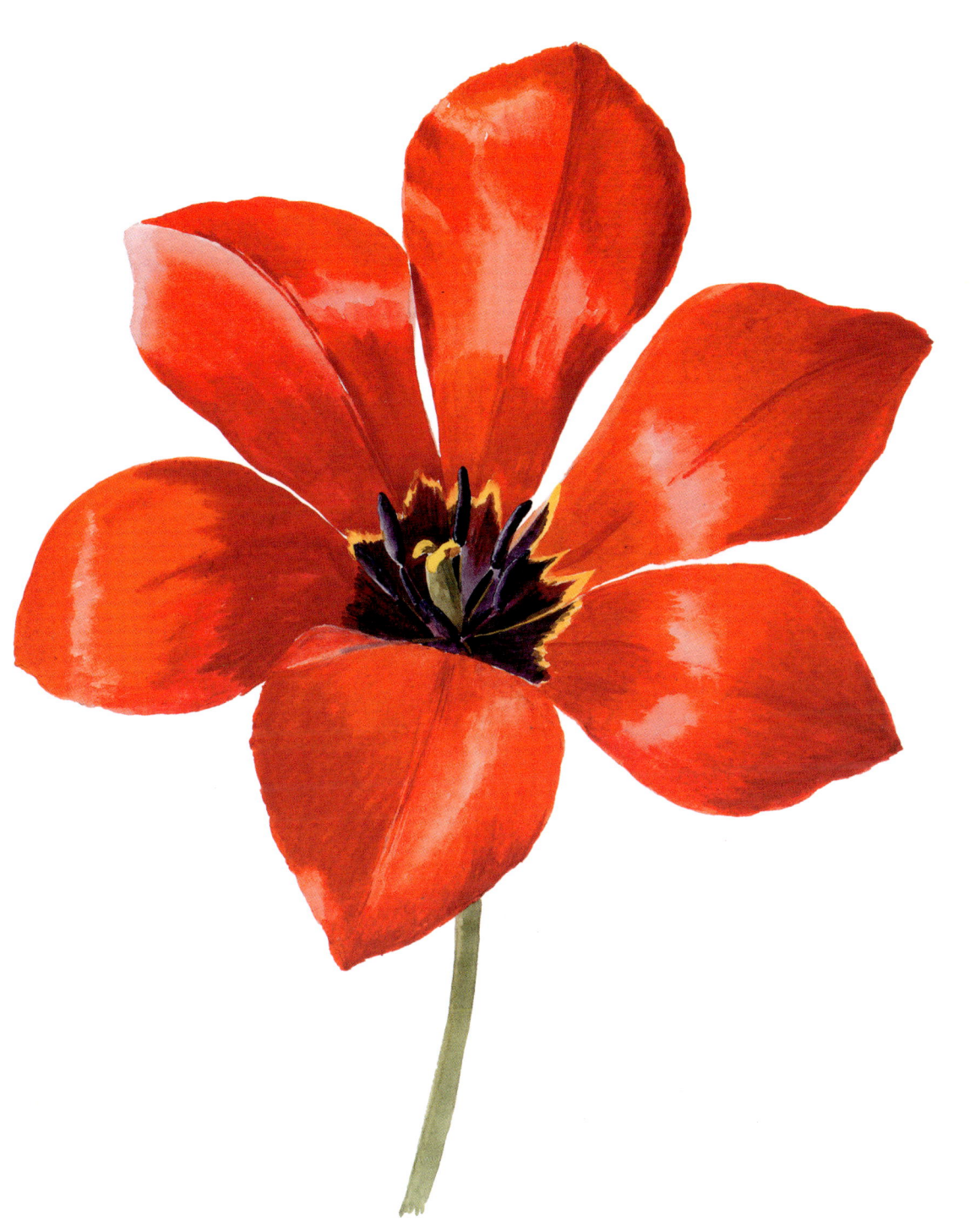

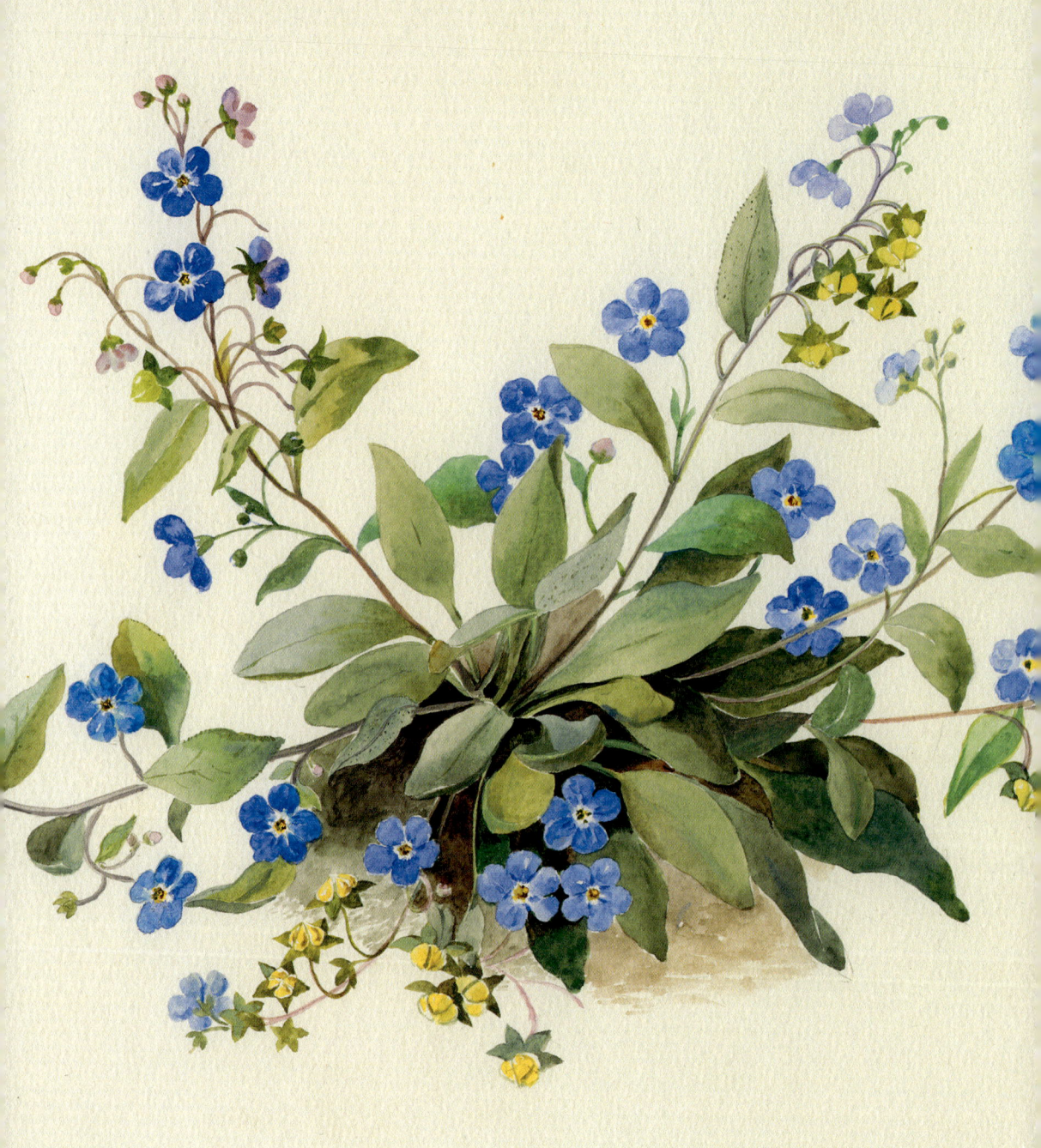

WEEK **14**

MARCH & APRIL

Monday **29**

First Day of Passover (Pesach) *Tuesday* **30**
Full Moon

Wednesday **31**

Maundy Thursday *Thursday* **1**

Good Friday *Friday* **2**
Holiday, UK, Canada, Australia
and New Zealand

Holiday, Australia *Saturday* **3**

Easter Day *Sunday* **4**

Omphalodes luciliae. Coloured drawing by Lilian Snelling, made for H.J. Elwes of Colesbourne in September 1915.

APRIL

WEEK **15**

5 Monday

Easter Monday
Holiday, UK (exc. Scotland), Republic of Ireland,
Canada, Australia and New Zealand
Seventh Day of Passover (Pesach)

6 Tuesday

Eighth Day of Passover (Pesach)
RHS London Greener Gardening Show
Last Quarter

7 Wednesday

RHS London Greener Gardening Show

8 Thursday

9 Friday

10 Saturday

11 Sunday

Five species of *Erythronium*: *E. hendersonii*, *E. johnstoni* [sic = *johnsoni*], *E. revolutum*, *E. hartwegi*, and *E. americanum*. Coloured drawing by Lilian Snelling, made for H.J. Elwes of Colesbourne in April 1915.

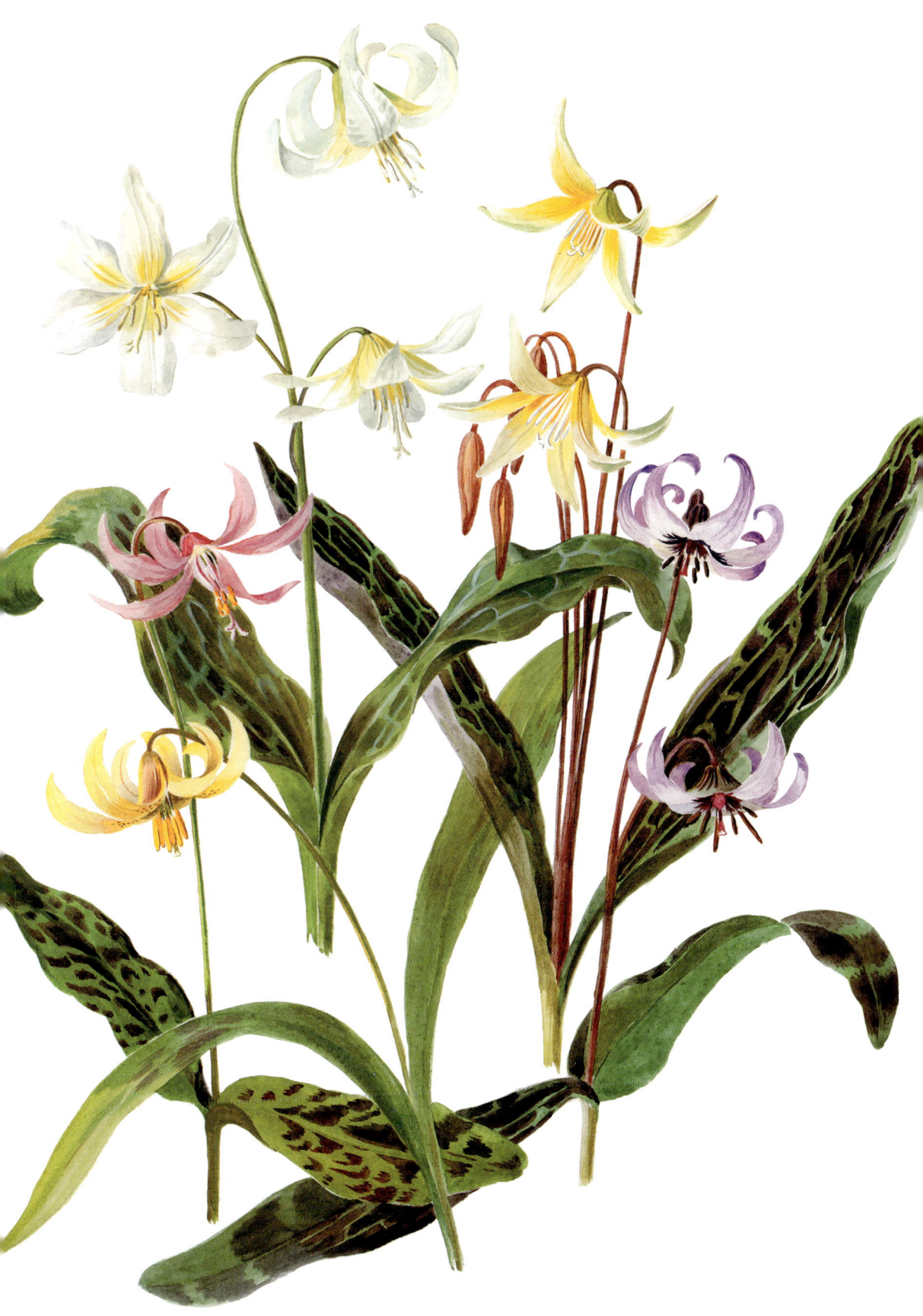

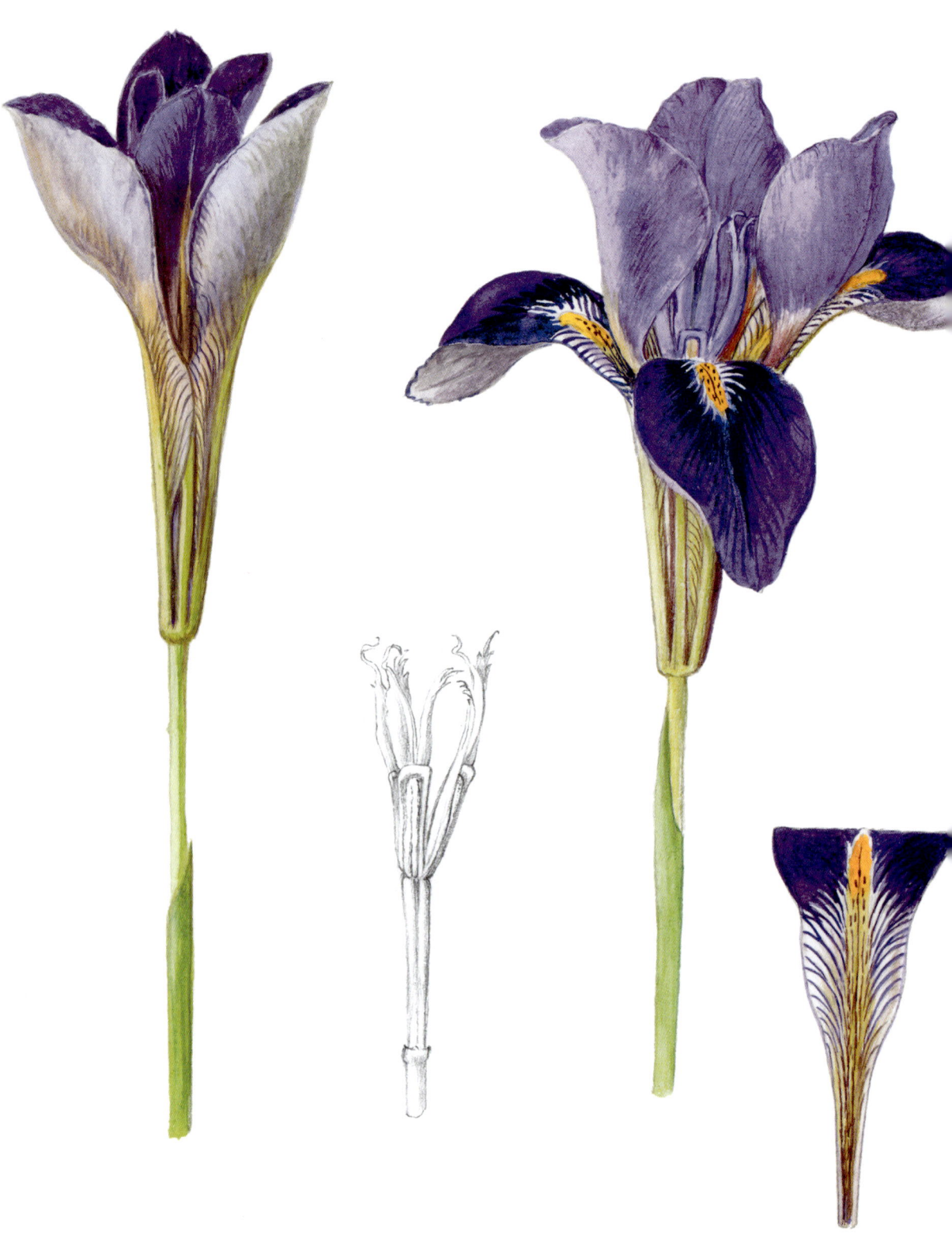

WEEK **16**

APRIL

Monday **12**

Tuesday **13**

New Moon

Wednesday **14**

Thursday **15**

RHS Show, Cardiff (subject to confirmation)

Friday **16**

RHS Show, Cardiff (subject to confirmation)
Cincinatti Flower & Garden Show, USA (subject to confirmation)

Saturday **17**

RHS Show, Cardiff (subject to confirmation)
Cincinatti Flower & Garden Show, USA (subject to confirmation)

Sunday **18**

Iris 'Mrs Barnard'. Coloured drawing, dated January 1952,
by Lilian Snelling, made from a specimen provided
by Mrs Stevenson of Balesmead.

APRIL

WEEK **17**

---

19 *Monday* — Cincinatti Flower & Garden Show, USA (subject to confirmation)

---

20 *Tuesday* — Cincinatti Flower & Garden Show, USA (subject to confirmation)

---

21 *Wednesday* — Birthday of Queen Elizabeth II
Cincinatti Flower & Garden Show, USA (subject to confirmation)
First Quarter

---

22 *Thursday* — Harrogate Spring Show (subject to confirmation)
Cincinatti Flower & Garden Show, USA (subject to confirmation)

---

23 *Friday* — St. George's Day
Cincinatti Flower & Garden Show, USA (subject to confirmation)

---

24 *Saturday* — Cincinatti Flower & Garden Show, USA (subject to confirmation)

---

25 *Sunday* — Anzac Day (Australia and New Zealand)
Cincinatti Flower & Garden Show, USA (subject to confirmation)

Fritillaria latifolia. Coloured drawing by Lilian Snelling, made for H.J. Elwes of Colesbourne in April 1915.

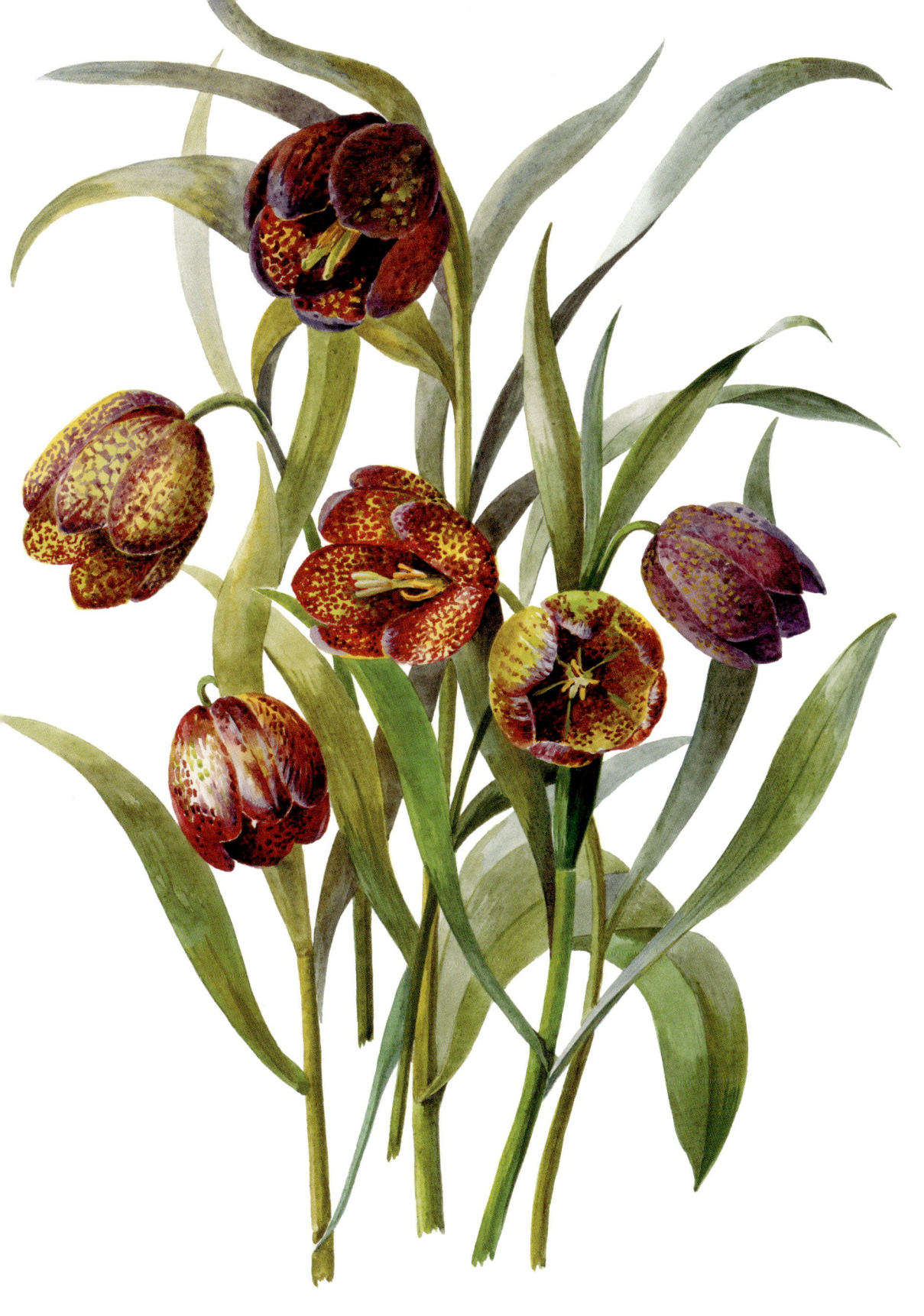

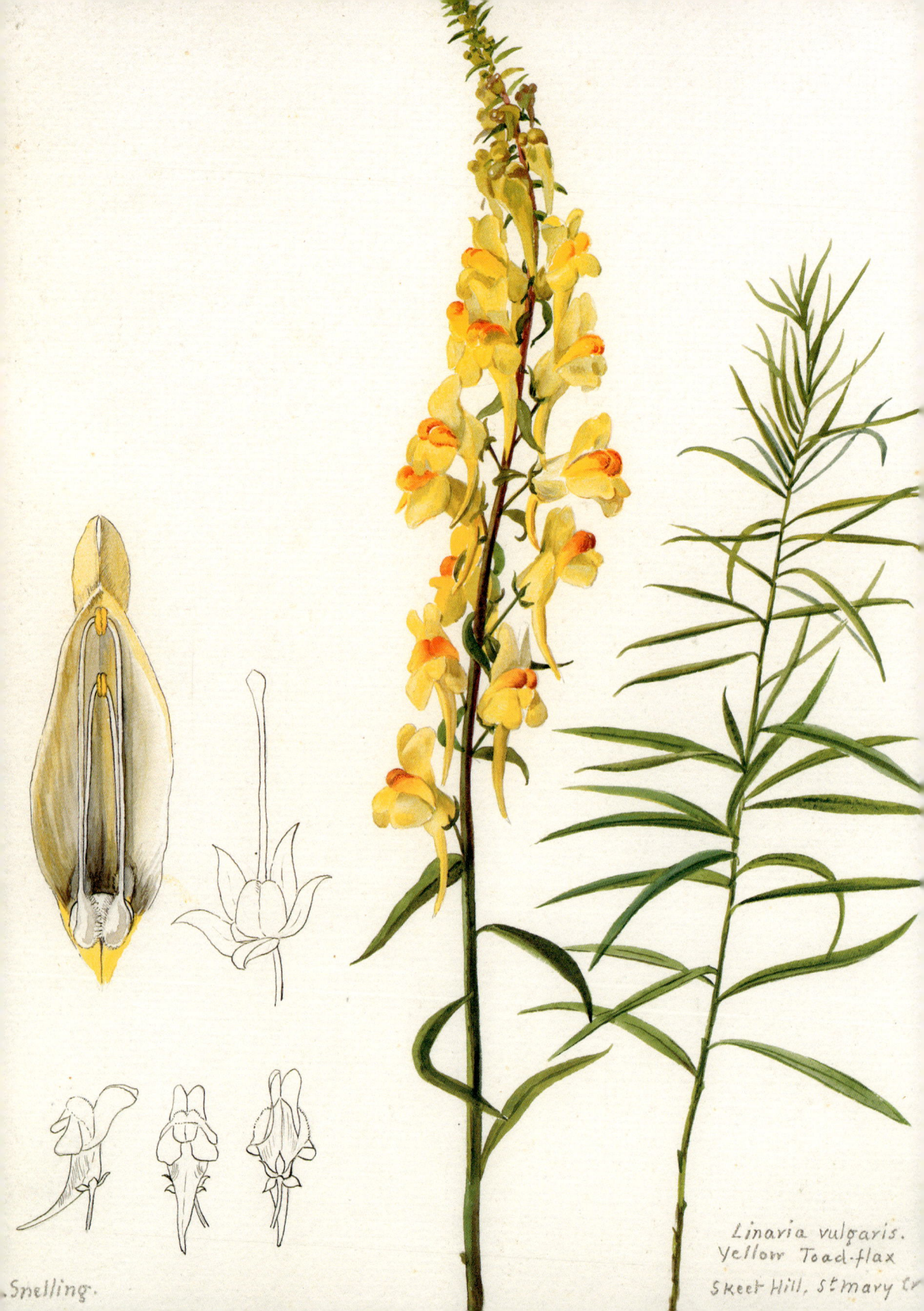

Snelling.

Linaria vulgaris.
Yellow Toad-flax
Skeet Hill, St Mary C

week **18**

APRIL & MAY

Holiday, Australia (Anzac Day)

Monday **26**

Tuesday **27**

Full Moon

Wednesday **28**

Thursday **29**

Friday **30**

Saturday **1**

Sunday **2**

Linaria vulgaris. Coloured drawing, undated, by Lilian Snelling.

MAY

WEEK **19**

3 *Monday* — Early Spring Bank Holiday, UK and Republic of Ireland

4 *Tuesday*

5 *Wednesday*

6 *Thursday* — Malvern Spring Gardening Show (RHS)
Last Quarter

7 *Friday* — Malvern Spring Gardening Show (RHS)

8 *Saturday* — Malvern Spring Gardening Show (RHS)

9 *Sunday* — Mother's Day, USA, Canada, Australia and New Zealand
Malvern Spring Gardening Show (RHS)

Paeonia clusii. Coloured drawing by Lilian Snelling, for a plate in Sir Frederick Stern's *Study of the genus Paeonia* (1946).

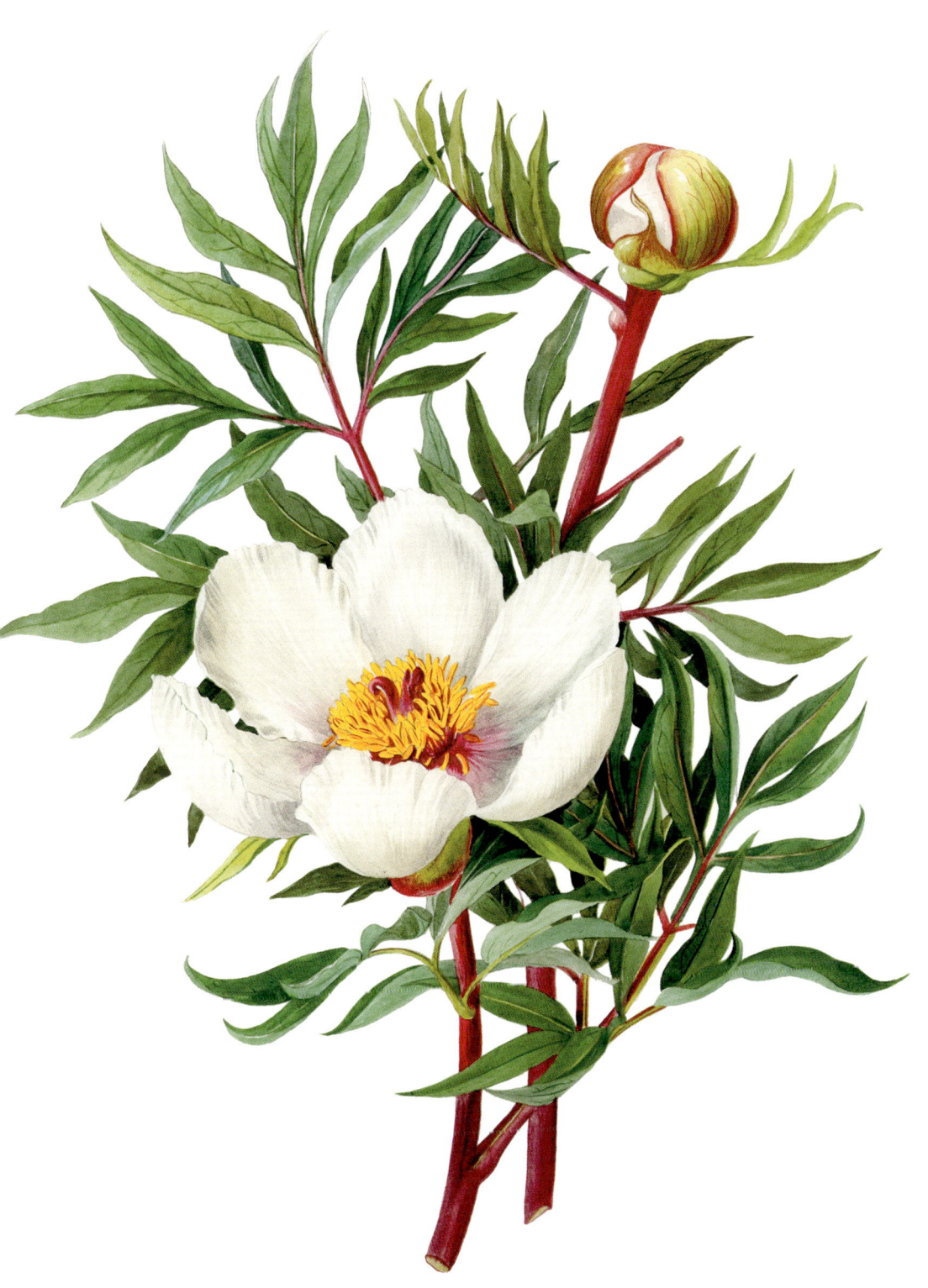

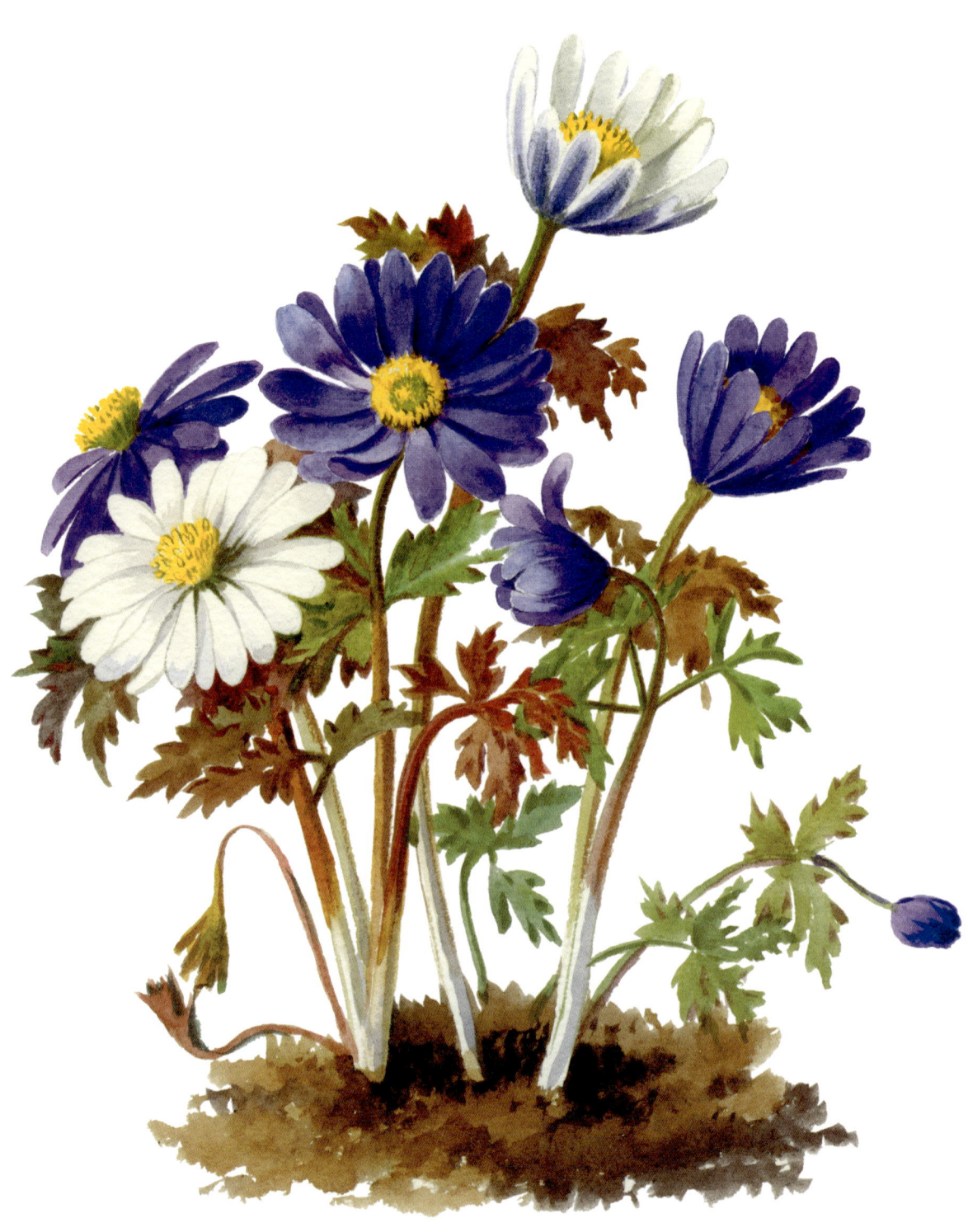

WEEK **20**

MAY

Monday **10**

Tuesday **11**

Wednesday **12**

Ascension Day — Thursday **13**

New Moon — Friday **14**

Saturday **15**

Sunday **16**

Anemone blanda var. *scythinica*, 3 April 1916. Coloured drawing by Lilian Snelling, made for H.J. Elwes of Colesbourne in April 1916.

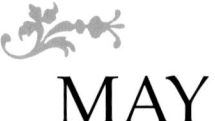

MAY

WEEK **21**

17 *Monday*

18 *Tuesday*

19 *Wednesday* — Feast of Weeks (Shavuot)

20 *Thursday* — *First Quarter*

21 *Friday*

22 *Saturday*

23 *Sunday* — Whit Sunday (Pentecost)

Paeonia anomala var. *intermedia*. Coloured drawing, dated May 1931, by Lilian Snelling, for a plate in Sir Frederick Stern's *Study of the genus Paeonia* (1946).

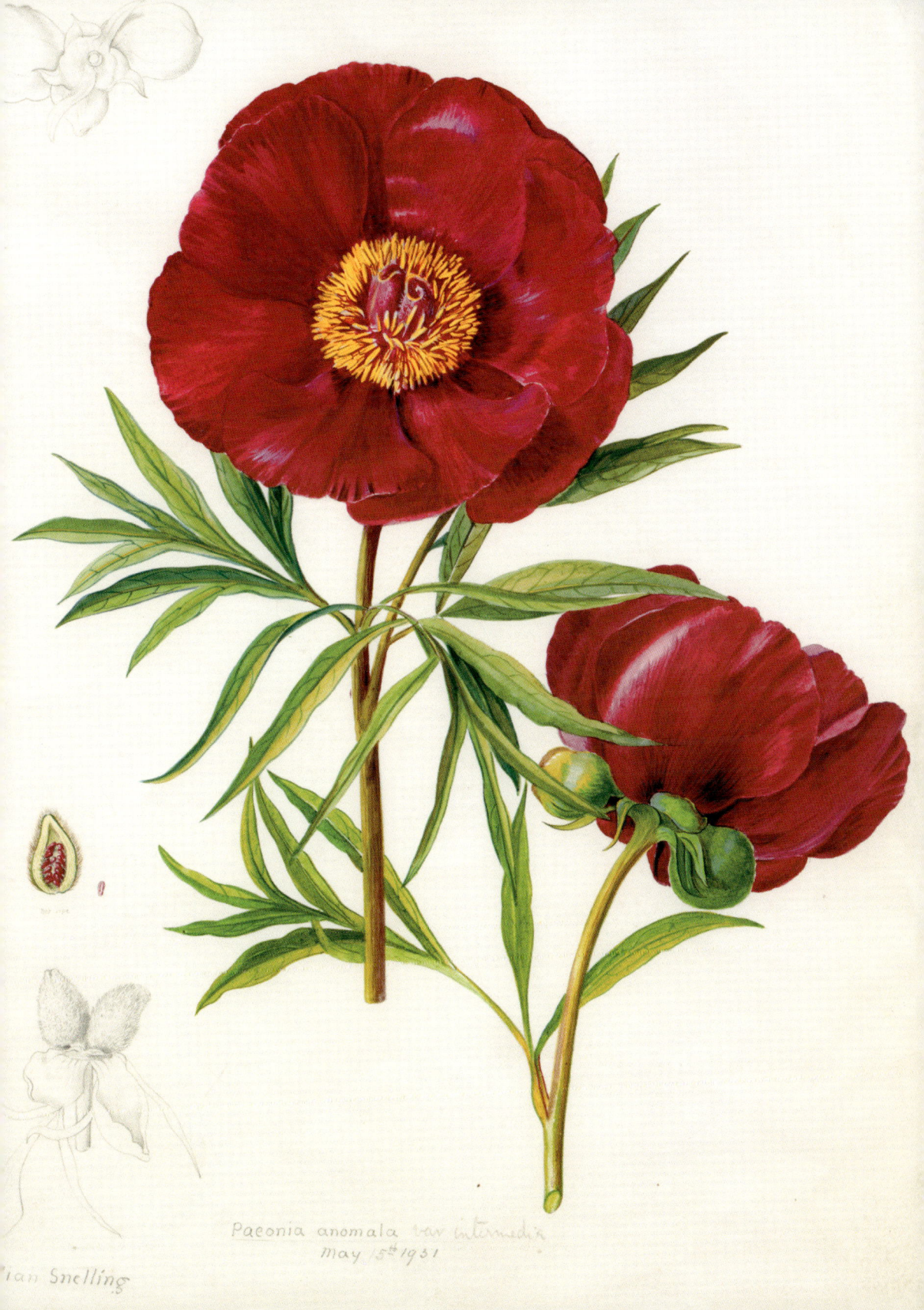

Paeonia anomala var intermedia
May 15th 1931

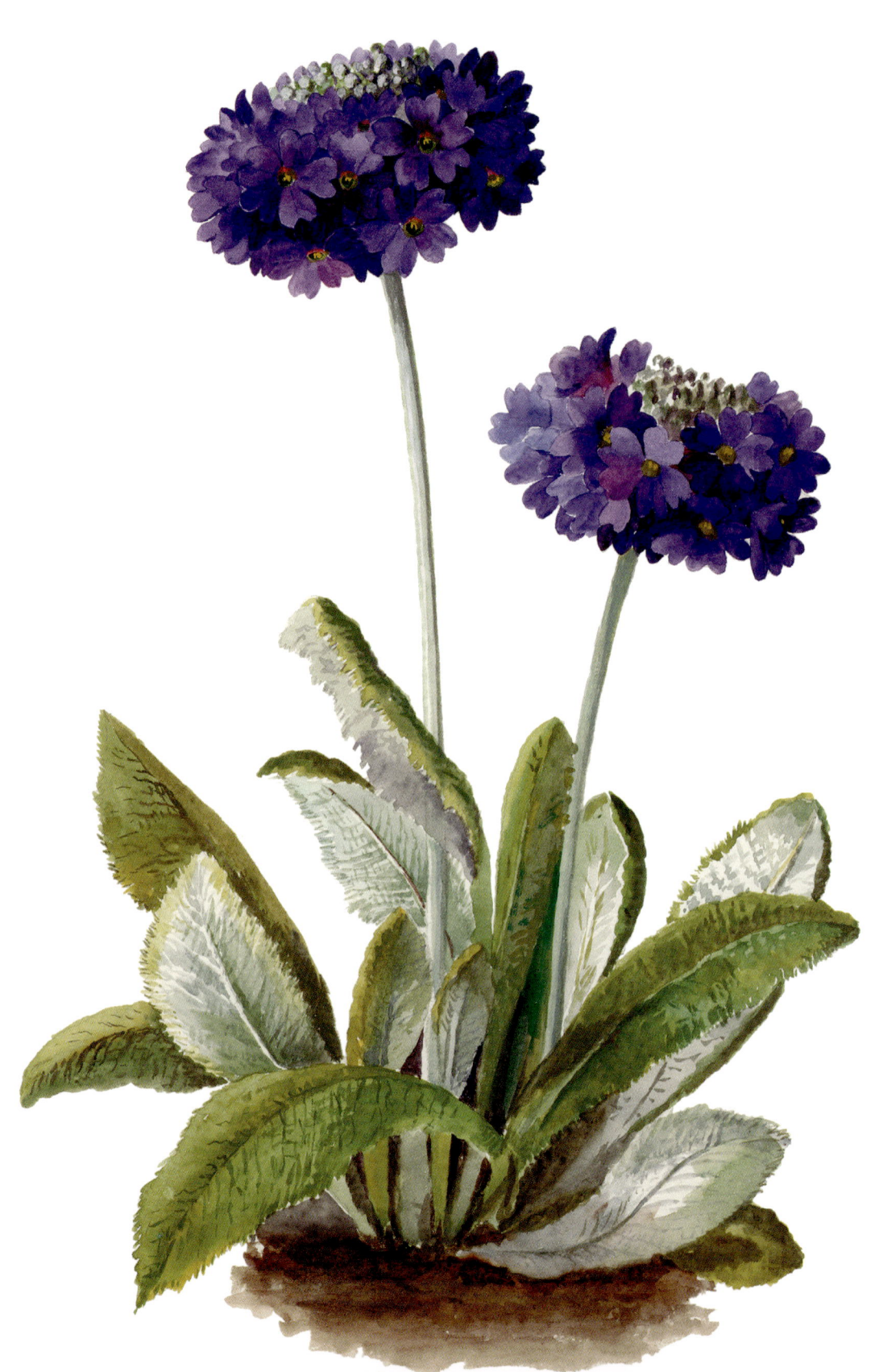

WEEK **22**

MAY

Holiday, Canada (Victoria Day) — *Monday* **24**

RHS Chelsea Flower Show — *Tuesday* **25**

RHS Chelsea Flower Show — *Wednesday* **26**

RHS Chelsea Flower Show
Full Moon — *Thursday* **27**

RHS Chelsea Flower Show — *Friday* **28**

RHS Chelsea Flower Show — *Saturday* **29**

Trinity Sunday — *Sunday* **30**

Primula capitata. Coloured drawing by Lilian Snelling, made for H.J. Elwes of Colesbourne in November 1915.

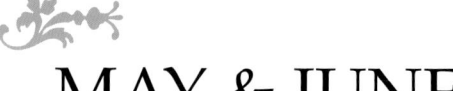

MAY & JUNE

WEEK **23**

31 *Monday* — Spring Bank Holiday, UK
Holiday, USA (Memorial Day)

1 *Tuesday*

2 *Wednesday* — Coronation Day

3 *Thursday* — Corpus Christi

4 *Friday* — Last Quarter

5 *Saturday*

6 *Sunday*

Bellis rotundifolia var. *caerulescens*. Coloured drawing, undated but made in the 1930s, by Lilian Snelling.

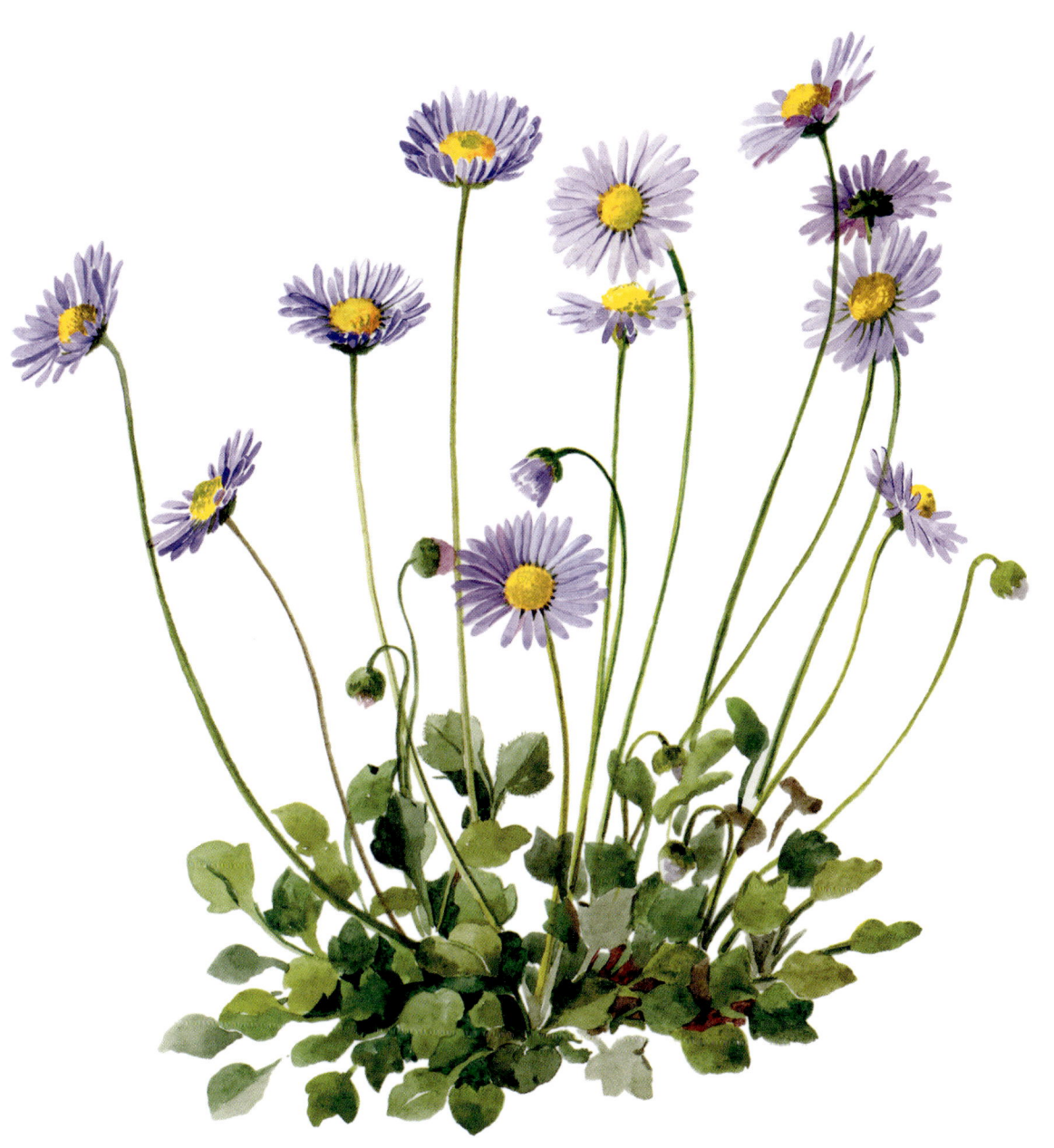

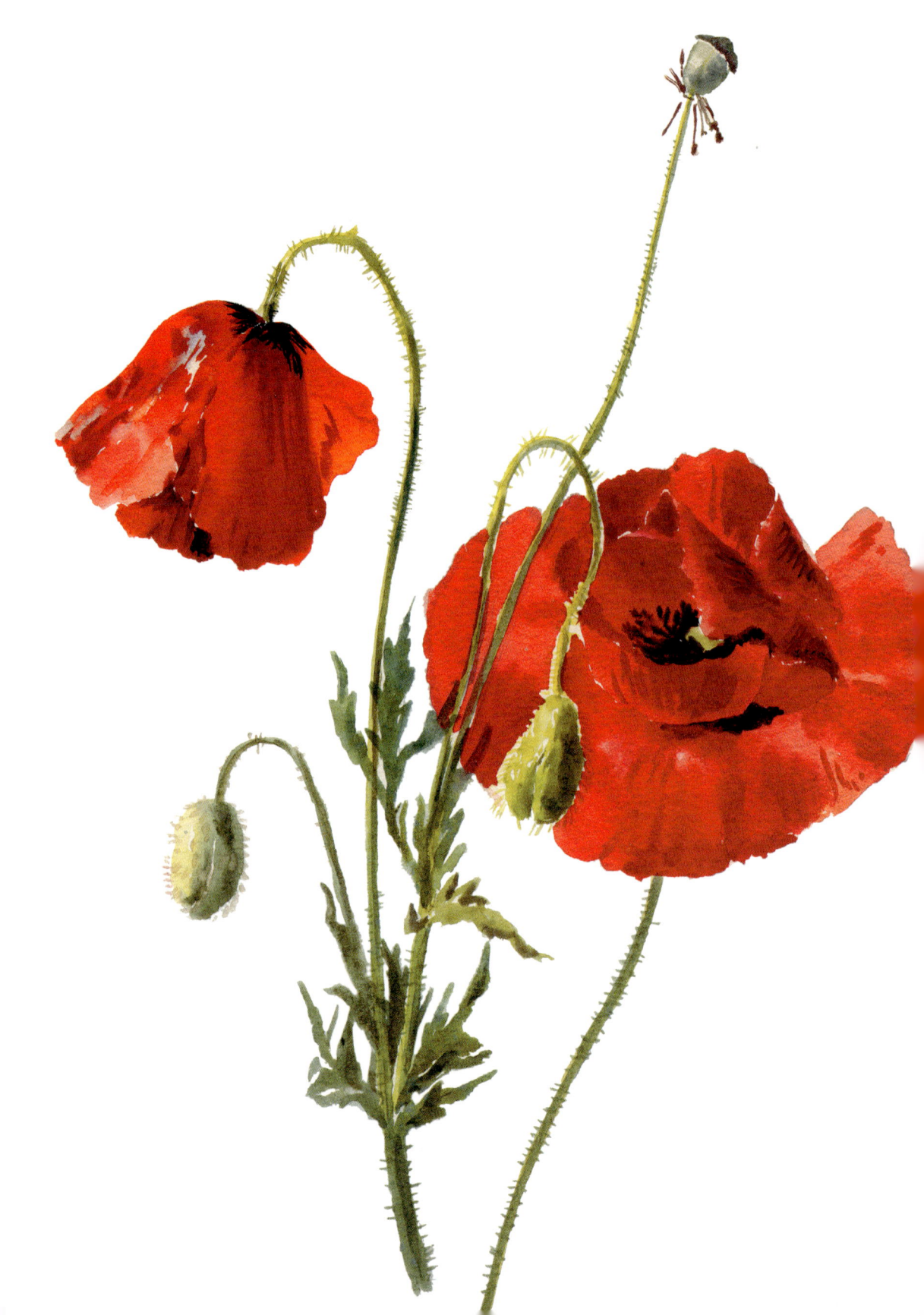

week **24**

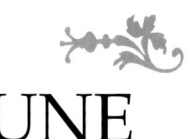

JUNE

Monday **7**

Holiday, Republic of Ireland
Holiday, New Zealand (Queen's Birthday)

Tuesday **8**

Wednesday **9**

RHS Wisley Music Festival
BBC Gardeners' World Live, Birmingham (subject to confirmation)

Thursday **10**

RHS Wisley Music Festival
BBC Gardeners' World Live, Birmingham (subject to confirmation)

Friday **11**

RHS Wisley Music Festival
BBC Gardeners' World Live, Birmingham (subject to confirmation)

Saturday **12**

RHS Wisley Music Festival
BBC Gardeners' World Live, Birmingham (subject to confirmation)
The Queen's Official Birthday (subject to confirmation)
New Moon

Sunday **13**

BBC Gardeners' World Live, Birmingham (subject to confirmation)

Papaver rhoeas. Coloured drawing, undated, by Lilian Snelling.

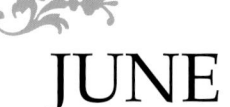

JUNE

WEEK **25**

---

14 *Monday*   Holiday, Australia (Queen's Birthday)

---

15 *Tuesday*

---

16 *Wednesday*

---

17 *Thursday*

---

18 *Friday*

---

19 *Saturday*   First Quarter

---

20 *Sunday*   Father's Day, UK, Canada and USA

Allium wallichii. Coloured drawing, undated, by Lilian Snelling.

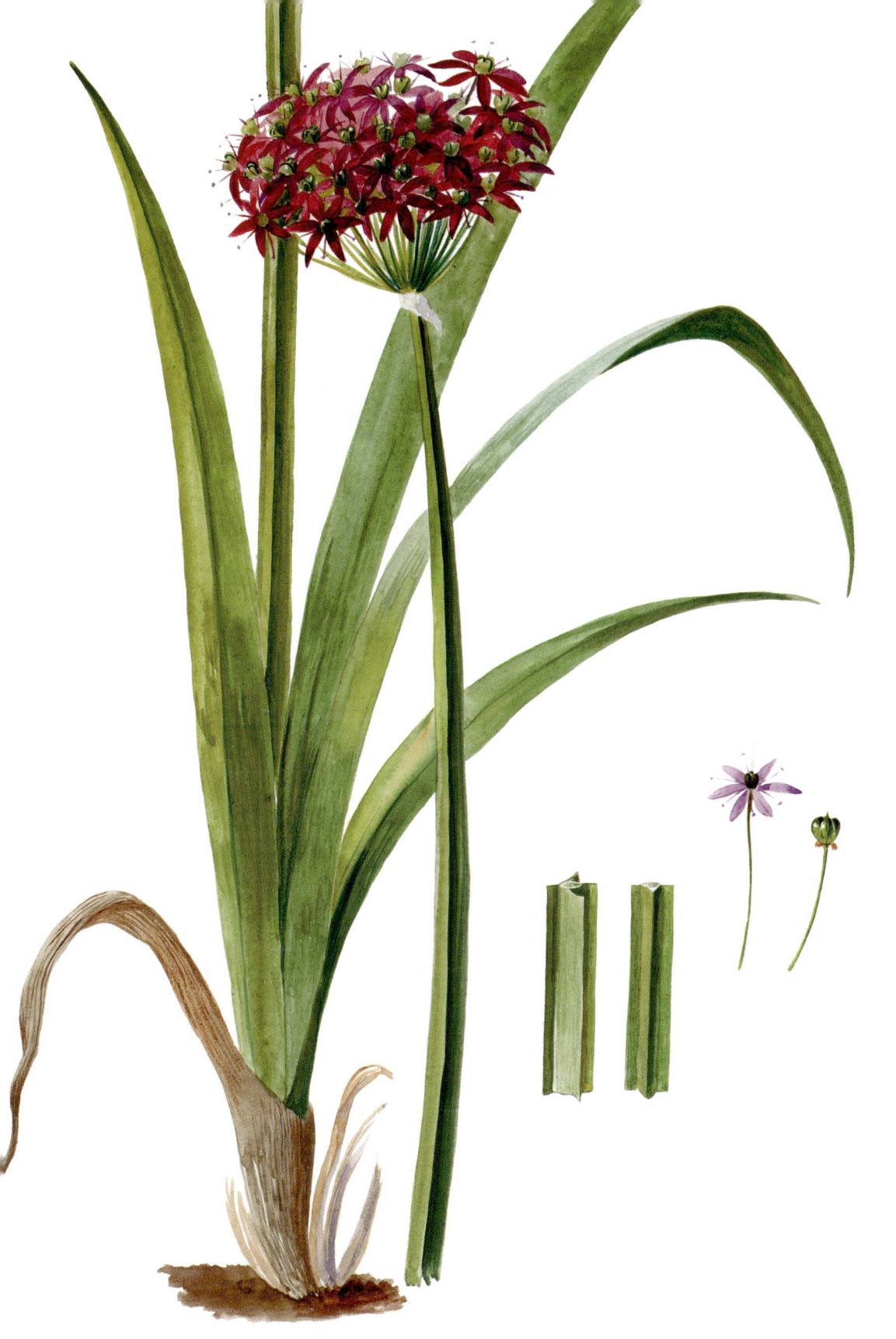

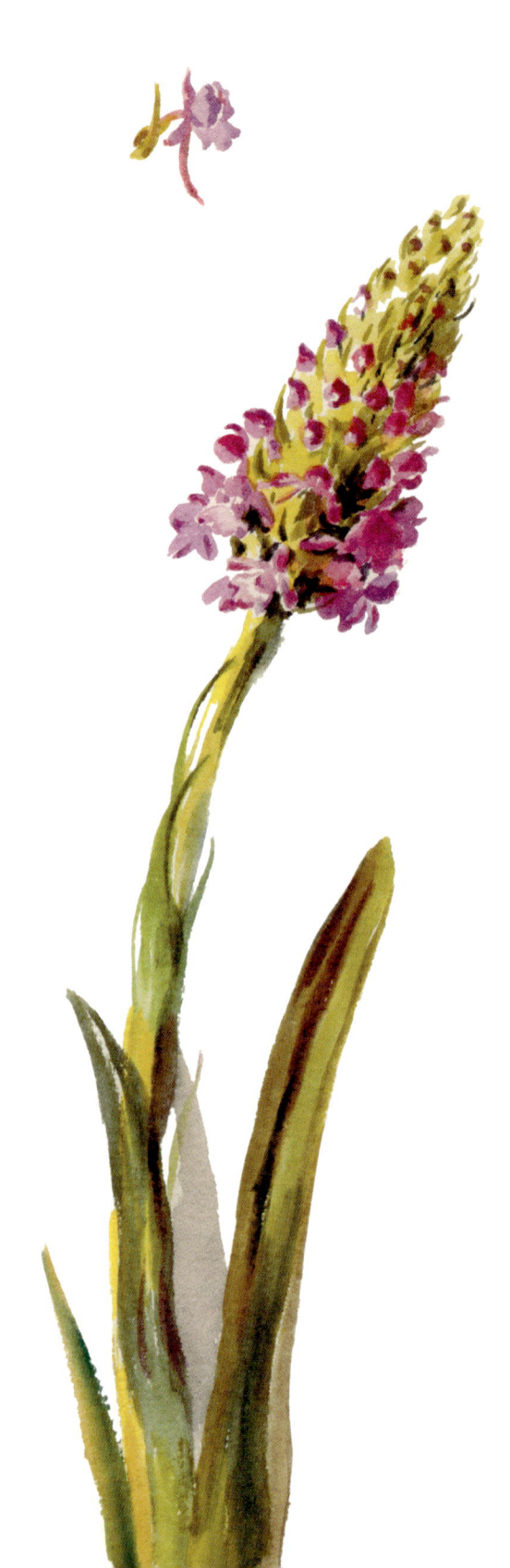

WEEK **26**

JUNE

Summer Solstice (Summer begins)   *Monday* **21**

Tuesday **22**

Wednesday **23**

Thursday **24**

Friday **25**

Full Moon   *Saturday* **26**

Sunday **27**

Orchis pyramidalis [now *Anacamptis pyramidalis*].
Coloured drawing, undated, by Lilian Snelling,
made from a specimen in Downe, Kent.

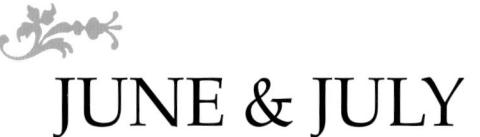

JUNE & JULY

WEEK **27**

28 *Monday*

29 *Tuesday*

30 *Wednesday*

1 *Thursday* — Holiday Canada (Canada Day)

2 *Friday*

3 *Saturday*

4 *Sunday* — Independence Day, USA
Last Quarter

Edraianthus serpyllifolium [sic = *serpyllifolius*; now *Campanula serpyllifolia*]. Coloured drawing, dated 1932, by Lilian Snelling, made from a specimen provided by Sir Frederick Stern.

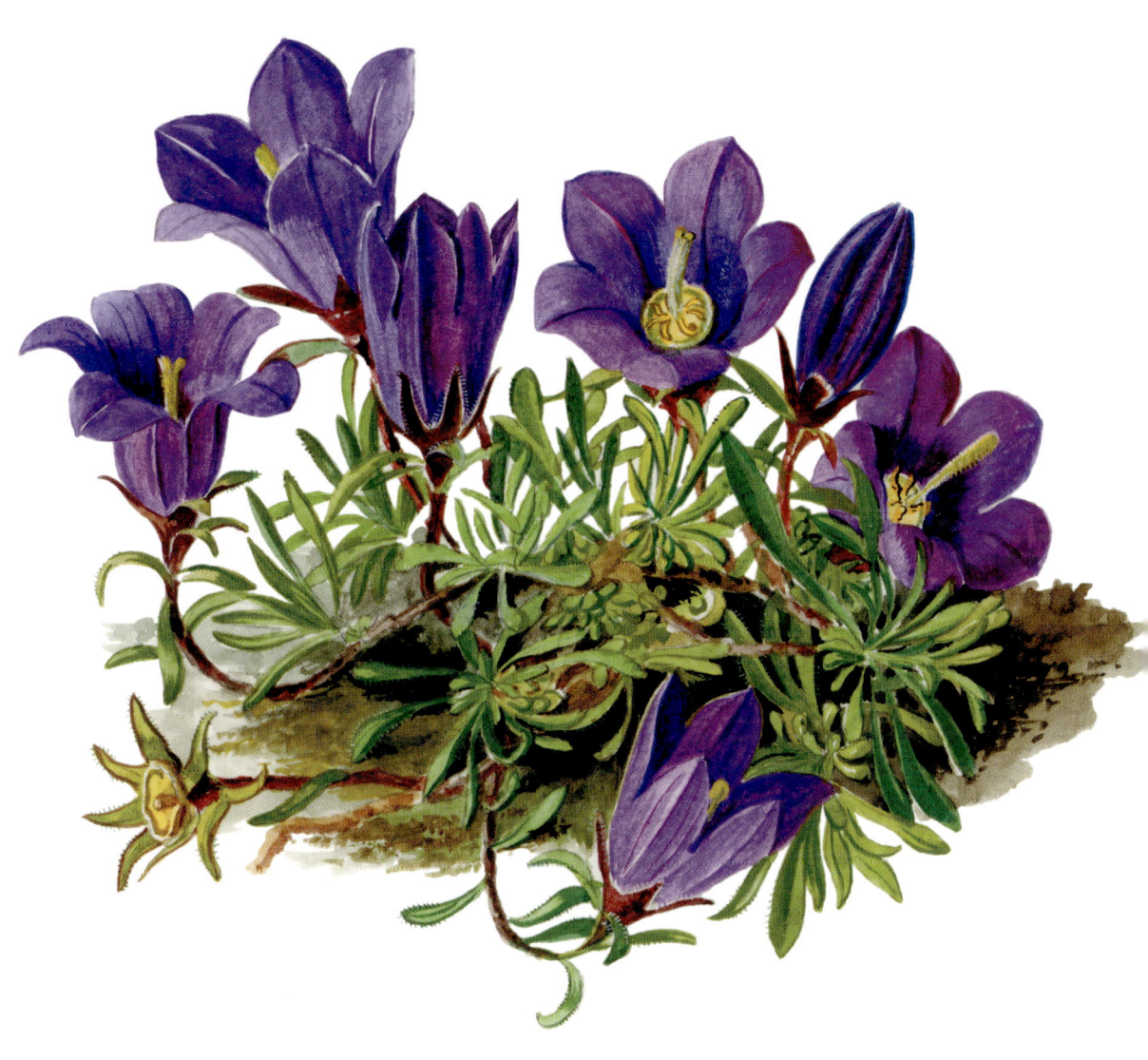

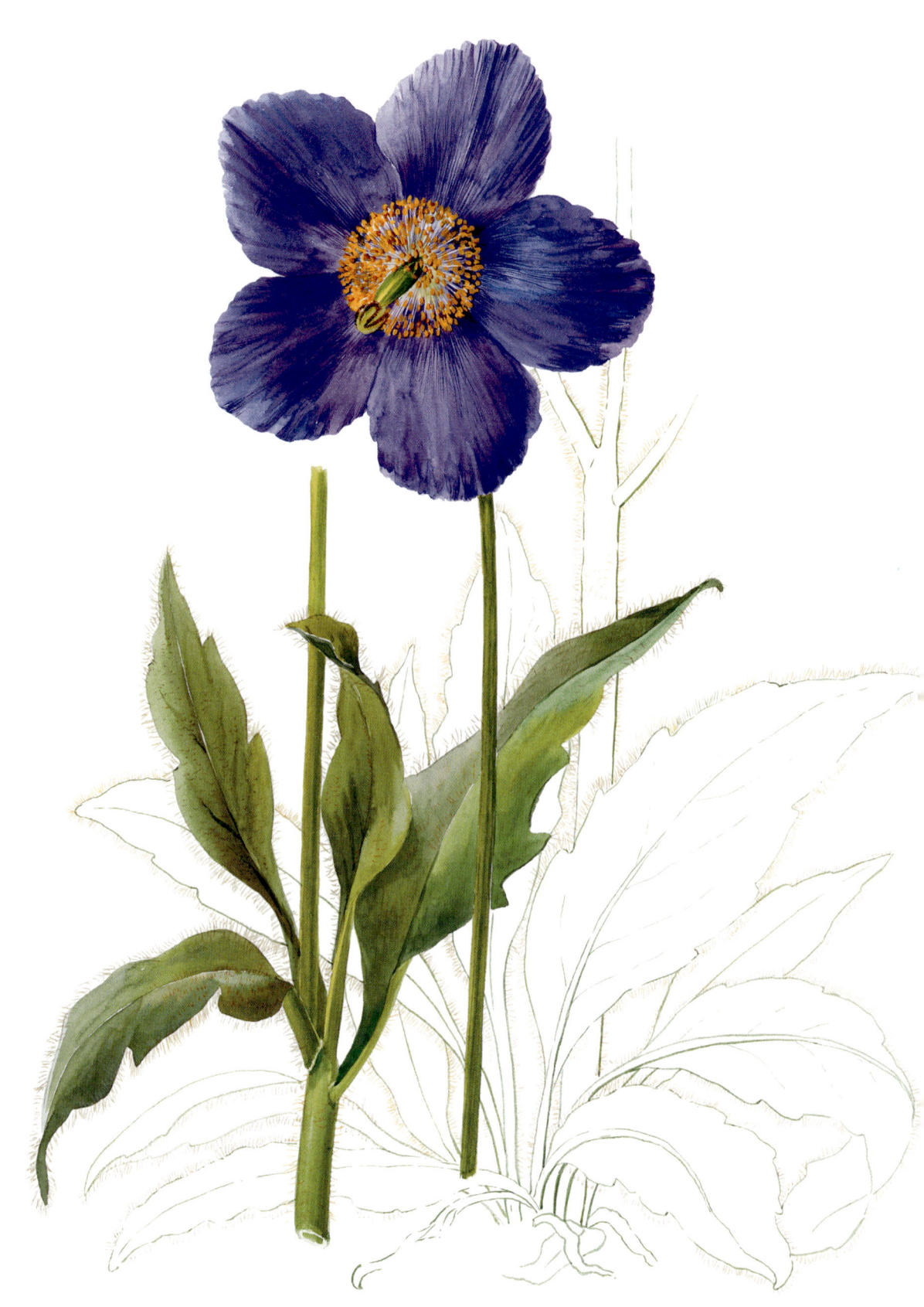

week **28**

JULY

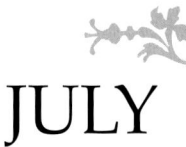

Holiday, USA (Independence Day) — *Monday* **5**

Tuesday **6**

RHS Hampton Court Palace Flower Show — *Wednesday* **7**

RHS Hampton Court Palace Flower Show — *Thursday* **8**

RHS Hampton Court Palace Flower Show — *Friday* **9**

RHS Hampton Court Palace Flower Show — *Saturday* **10**

RHS Hampton Court Palace Flower Show
New Moon — *Sunday* **11**

Meconopsis grandis. Coloured drawing by Lilian Snelling, made while working at the Edinburgh Botanic Garden in June 1916.

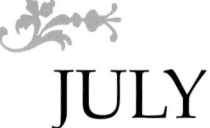

JULY

WEEK **29**

12 *Monday*   Holiday, Northern Ireland (Battle of the Boyne)

13 *Tuesday*

14 *Wednesday*

15 *Thursday*   St. Swithin's Day

16 *Friday*

17 *Saturday*

18 *Sunday*   First Quarter

Carduus sp. Coloured drawing by Lilian Snelling, made from a specimen found at Corstorphine, while working at the Edinburgh Botanic Garden in 1918.

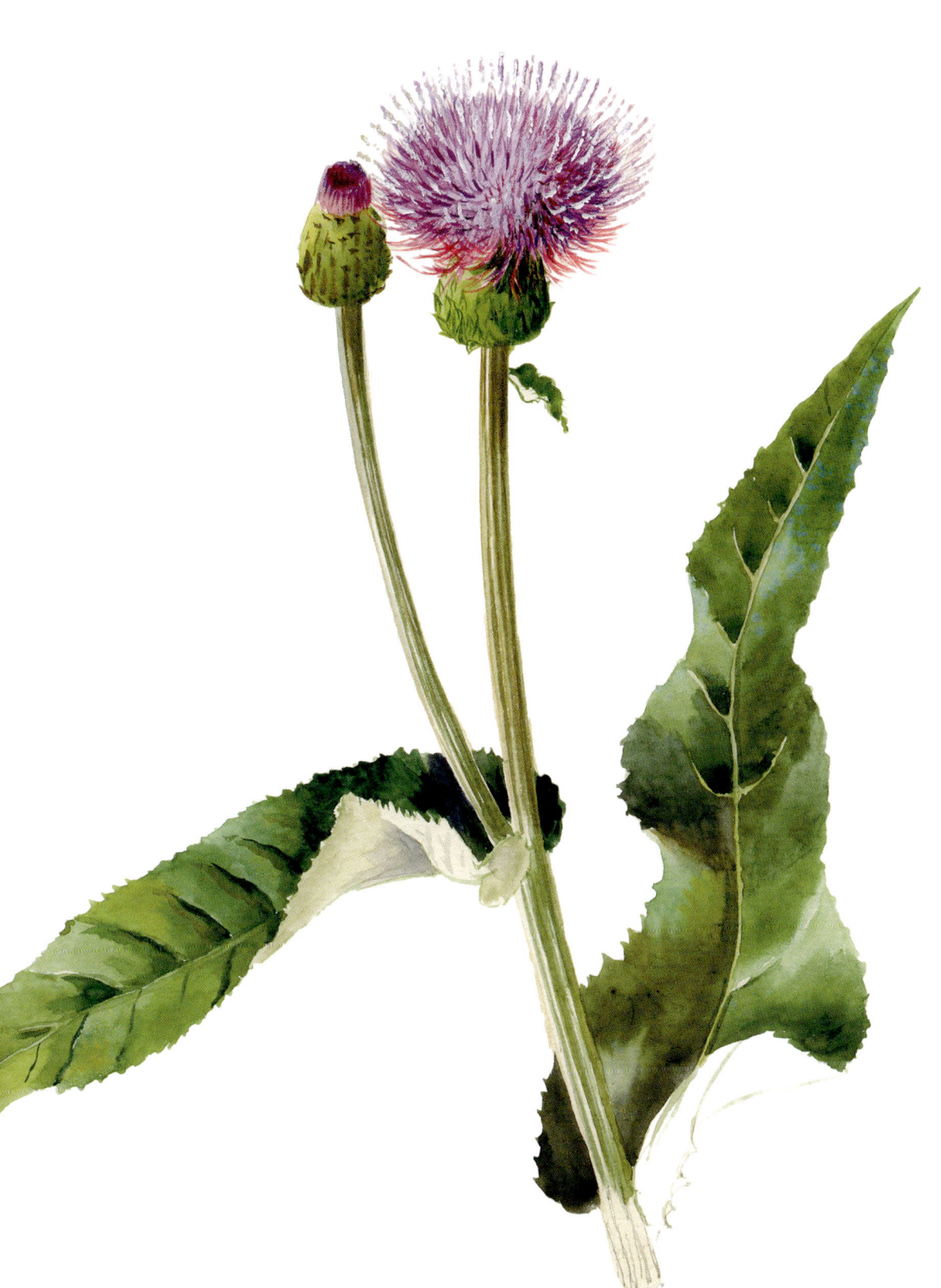

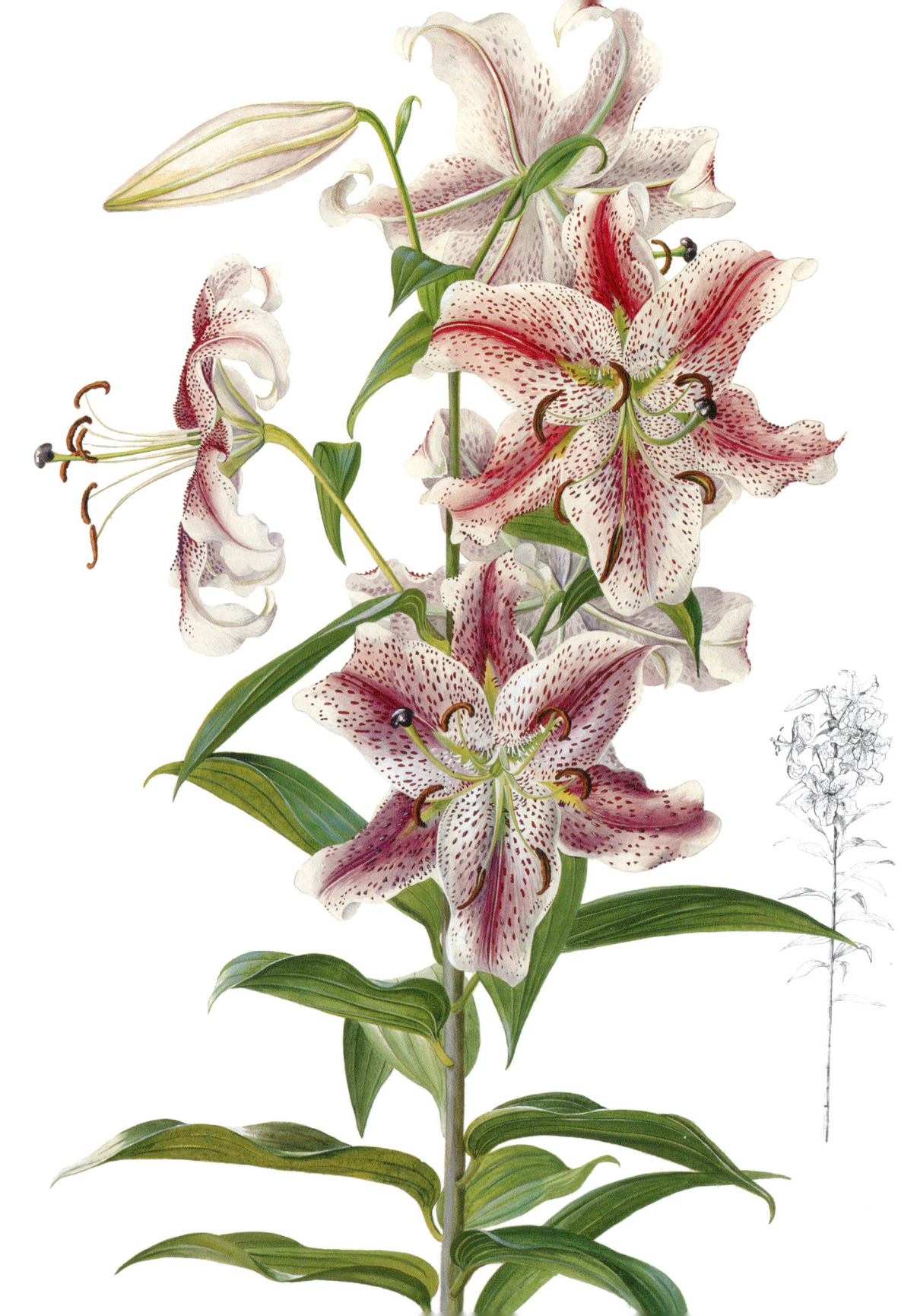

WEEK **30**

JULY

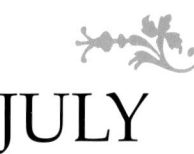

Monday **19**

Tuesday **20**

RHS Show at Tatton Park | *Wednesday* **21**

RHS Show at Tatton Park | *Thursday* **22**

RHS Show at Tatton Park | *Friday* **23**

RHS Show at Tatton Park | *Saturday* **24**

RHS Show at Tatton Park | *Sunday* **25**

Lilium × parkmanni. Coloured drawing, undated, by Lilian Snelling.

JULY & AUGUST

WEEK **31**

26 *Monday* — *Full Moon*

27 *Tuesday*

28 *Wednesday*

29 *Thursday*

30 *Friday*

31 *Saturday*

1 *Sunday*

Verbascum nigrum. Coloured drawing, undated, by Lilian Snelling.

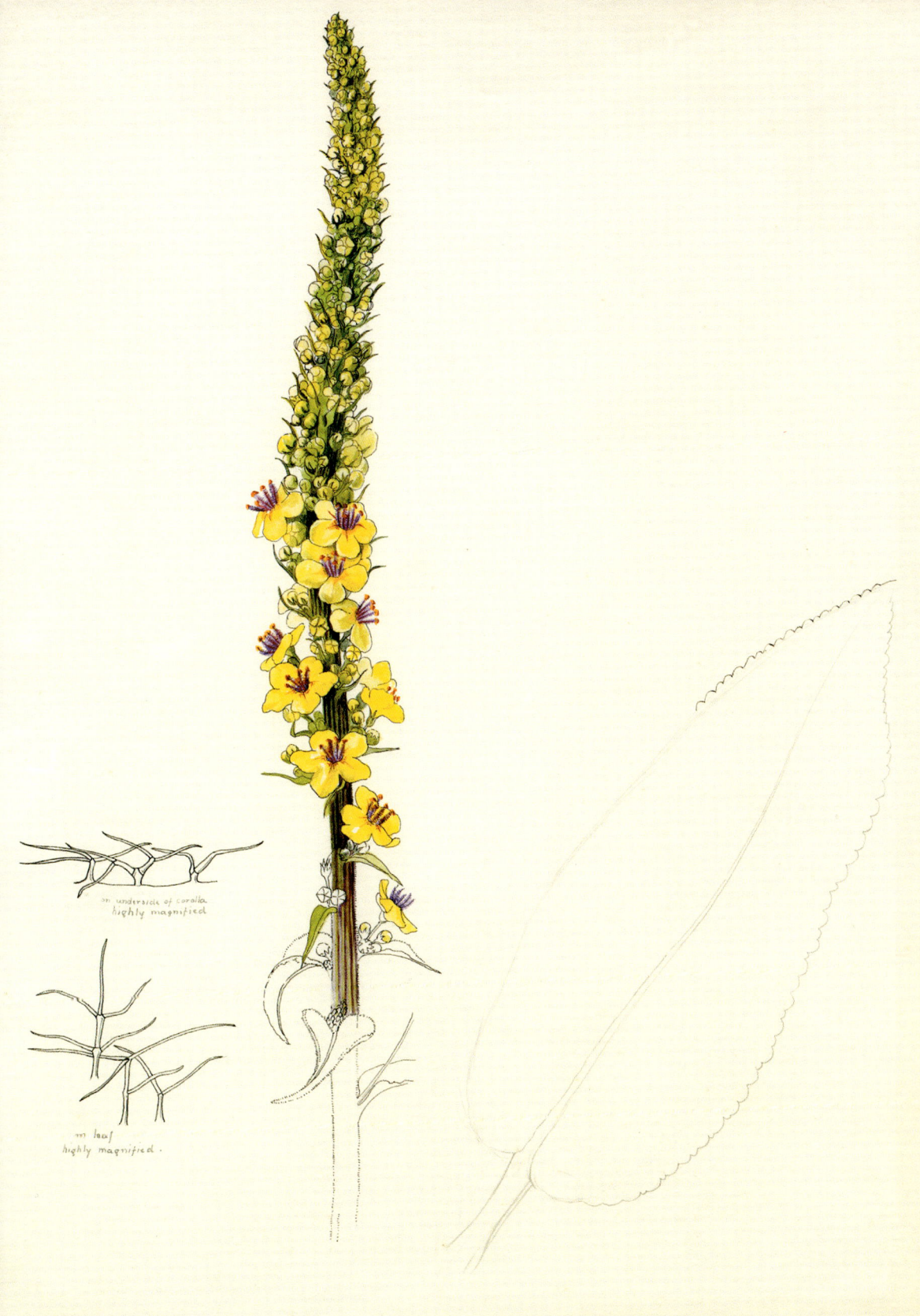

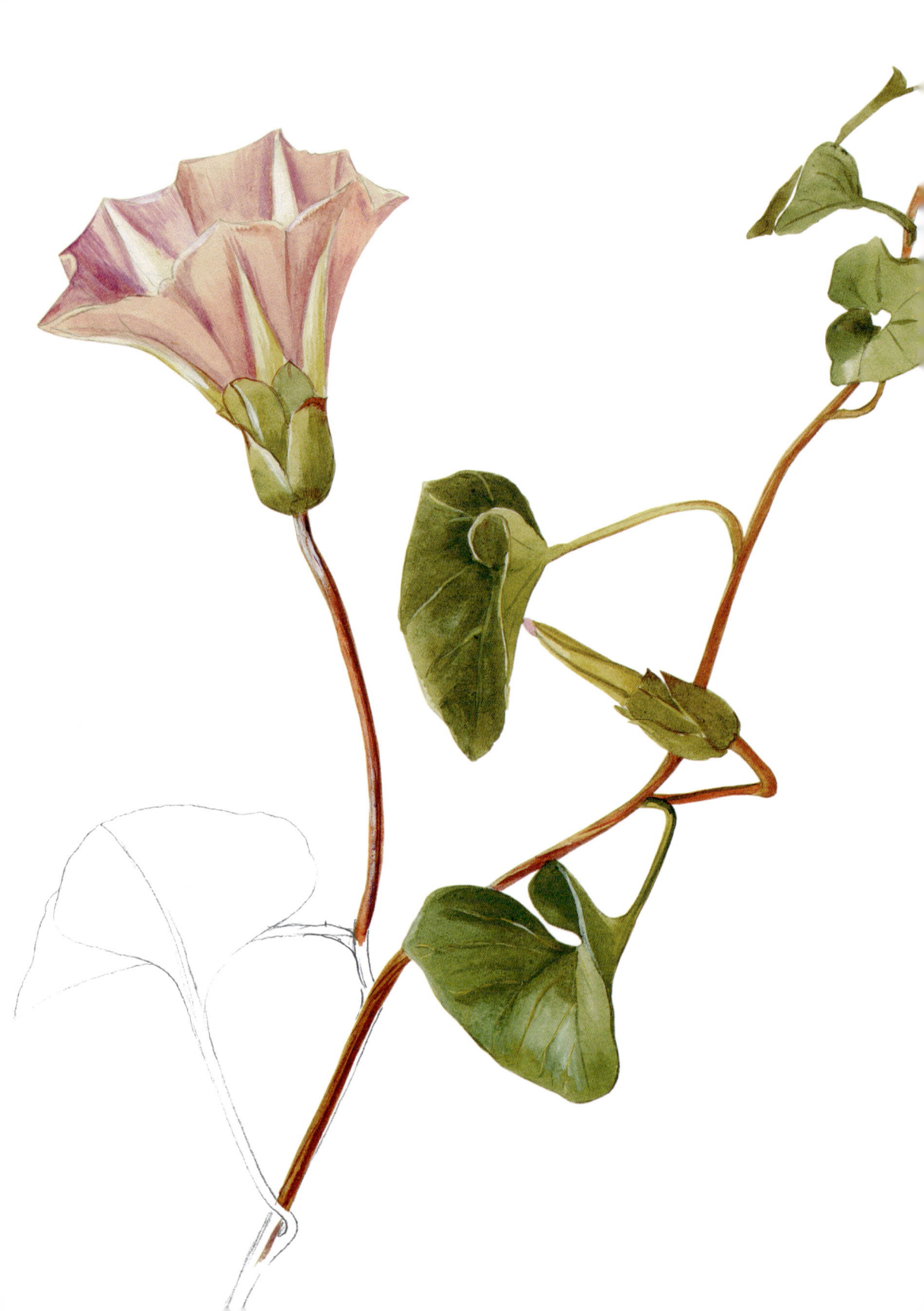

WEEK **32**

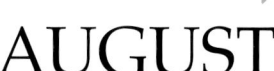

AUGUST

Summer Bank Holiday, Scotland
Holiday, Republic of Ireland

Monday **2**

Last Quarter

Tuesday **3**

Wednesday **4**

Thursday **5**

Friday **6**

Saturday **7**

Sunday **8**

Convolvulus arvensis. Coloured drawing, undated, by Lilian Snelling, made from a specimen found on the Isle of Wight.

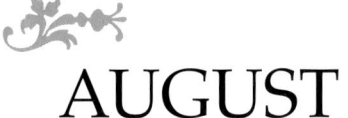

AUGUST

WEEK **33**

9 *Monday*

10 *Tuesday* — New Moon

11 *Wednesday* — First Day of Ramadân (subject to sighting of the moon)

12 *Thursday*

13 *Friday*

14 *Saturday*

15 *Sunday*

Kniphofia galpinii. Original drawing by Lilian Snelling, for plate 8928 of *Curtis's Botanical Magazine* (1938).

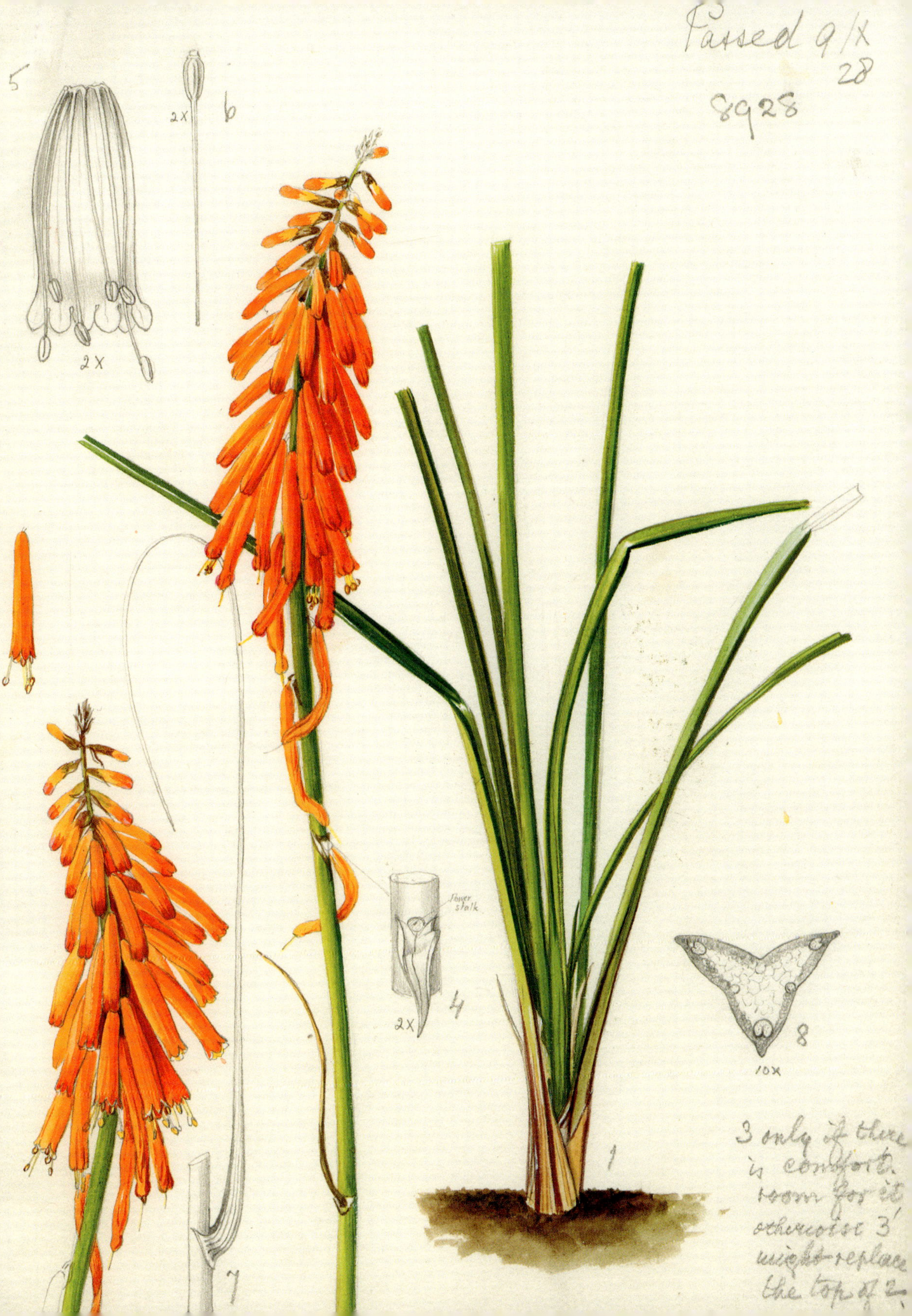

Passed 9/X 28

8928

3 only if there is comfort. room for it otherwise 3' might replace the top of 2

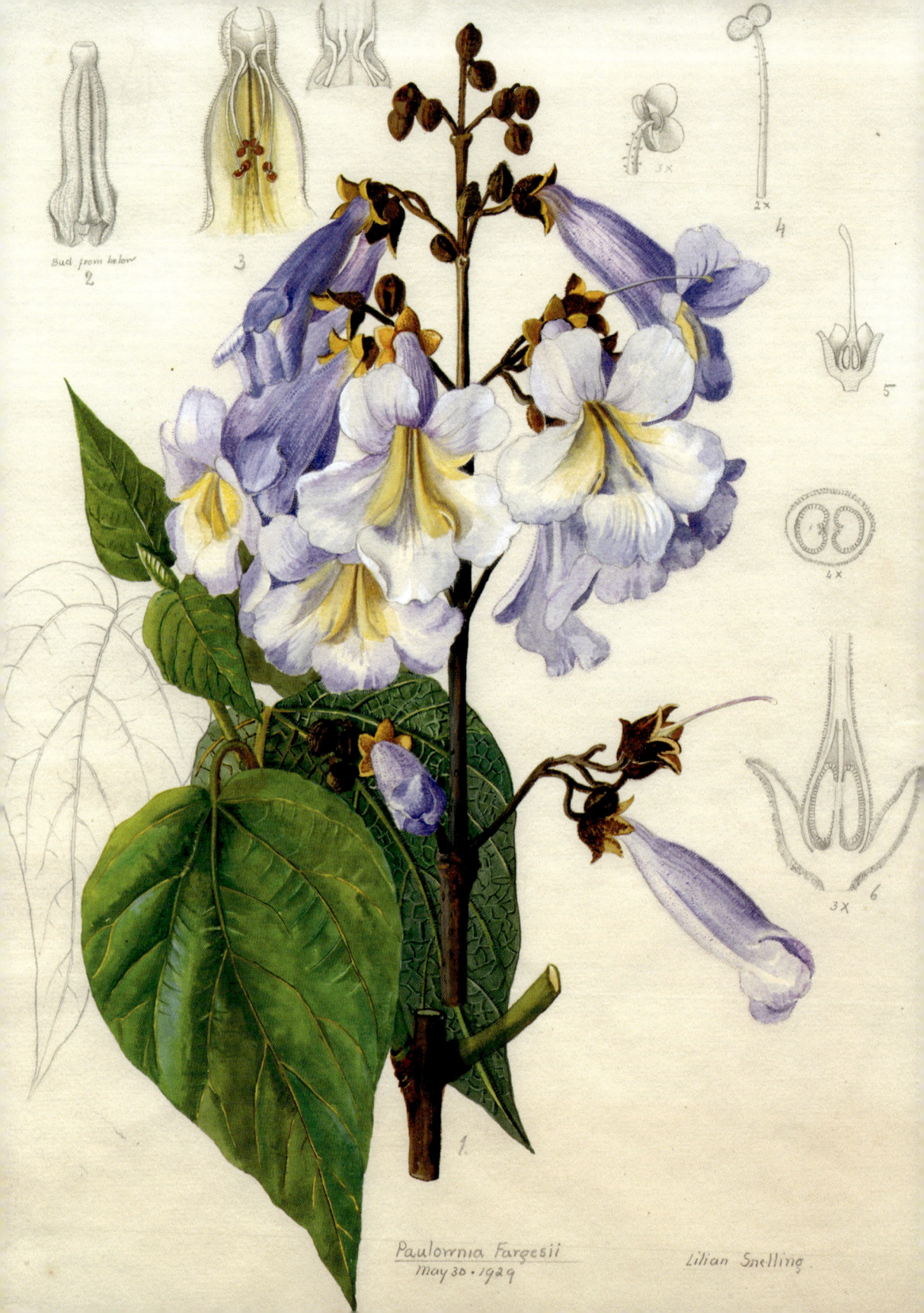

Paulownia Fargesii
May 30 · 1929

Lilian Snelling

WEEK **34**

First Quarter

Monday **16**

Tuesday **17**

Wednesday **18**

Thursday **19**

Friday **20**

Saturday **21**

Sunday **22**

AUGUST

Paulownia tomentosa 'Lilacina'. Original drawing by Lilian Snelling, described by her as *Paulownia fargesii*, for plate 8926–7 of *Curtis's Botanical Magazine* (1938), where it bore the name *Paulownia lilacina*.

AUGUST

WEEK **35**

23 *Monday*

24 *Tuesday* *Full Moon*

25 *Wednesday*

26 *Thursday*

27 *Friday*

28 *Saturday*

29 *Sunday*

Lathyrus sylvestris. Coloured drawing, undated, by Lilian Snelling.

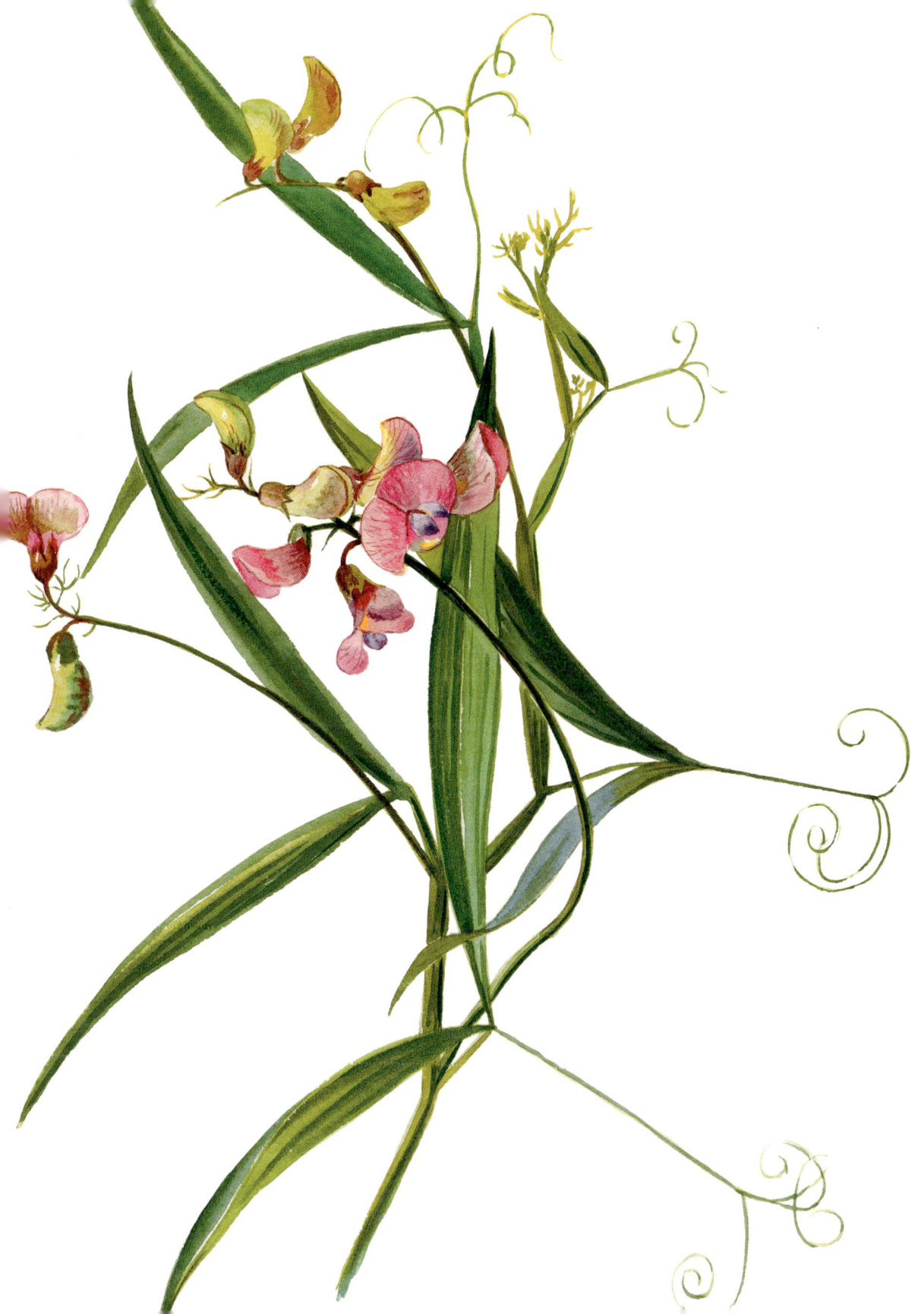

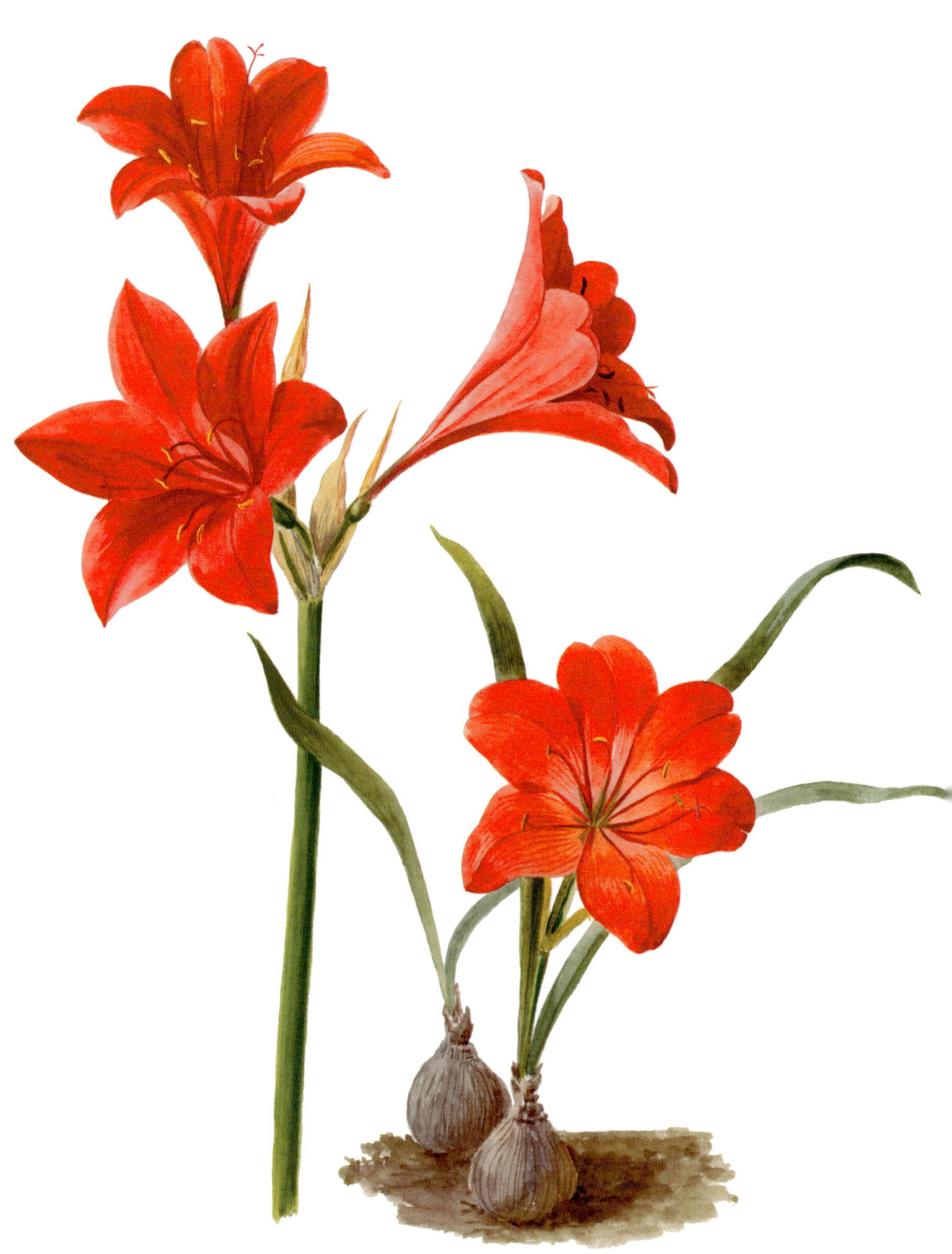

week **36**

AUGUST & SEPTEMBER

Summer Bank Holiday UK (exc. Scotland)   *Monday* **30**

Tuesday **31**

Last Quarter   *Wednesday* **1**

Thursday **2**

Friday **3**

Saturday **4**

Father's Day, Australia and New Zealand   *Sunday* **5**

Vallota × *gastronema*. Coloured drawing, dated September 1915, by Lilian Snelling, of a hybrid raised at Colesbourne by H.J. Elwes.

SEPTEMBER

WEEK **37**

6 *Monday*

Holiday, USA (Labor Day)
Holiday, Canada (Labour Day)

7 *Tuesday*

8 *Wednesday*

New Moon

9 *Thursday*

Jewish New Year (Rosh Hashanah)
Eid al-Fitr, Ramadân ends (subject to sighting of the moon)

10 *Friday*

11 *Saturday*

12 *Sunday*

Anemonopsis macrophylla. Coloured drawing by Lilian Snelling, made for H.J. Elwes of Colesbourne in August 1915.

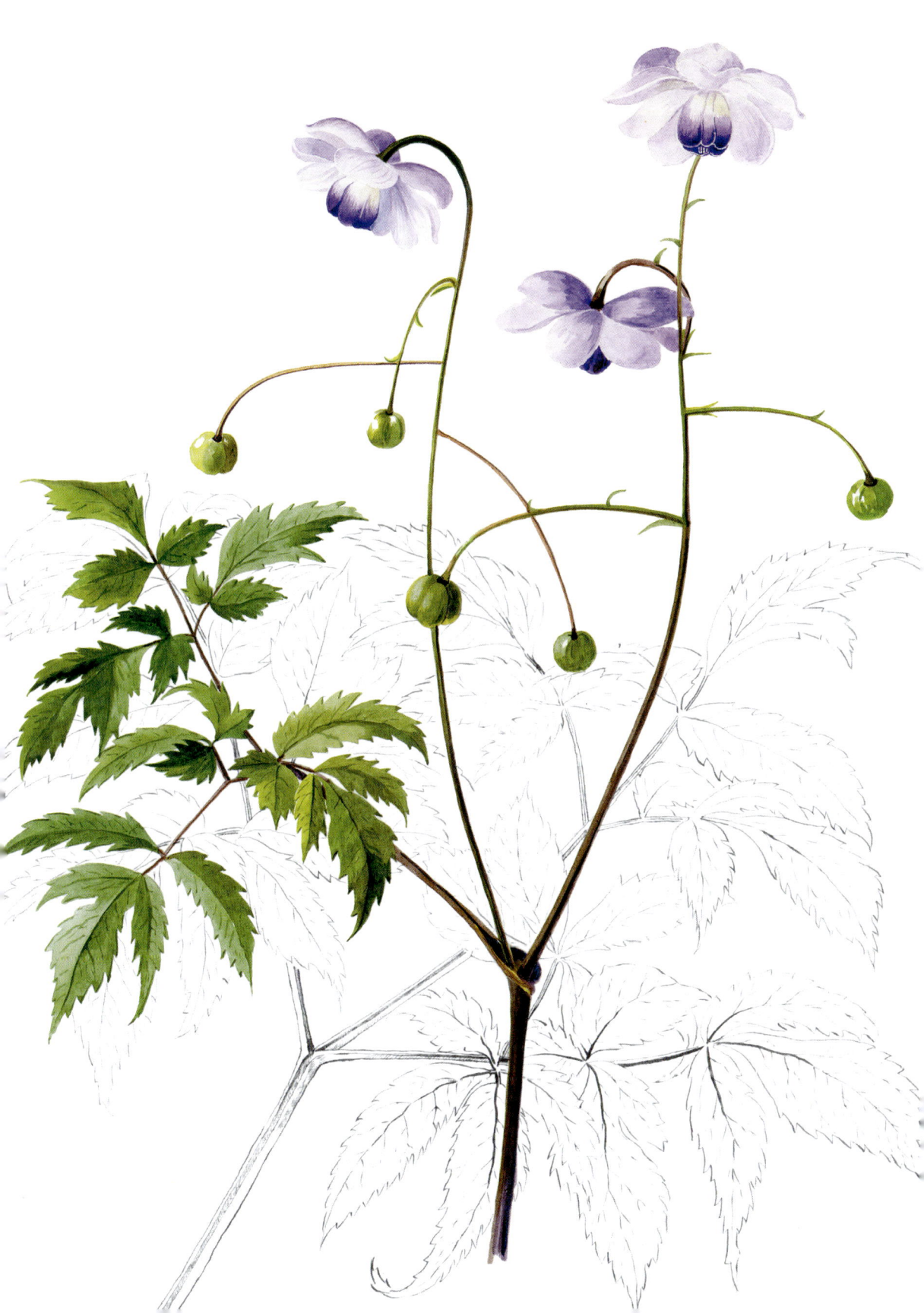

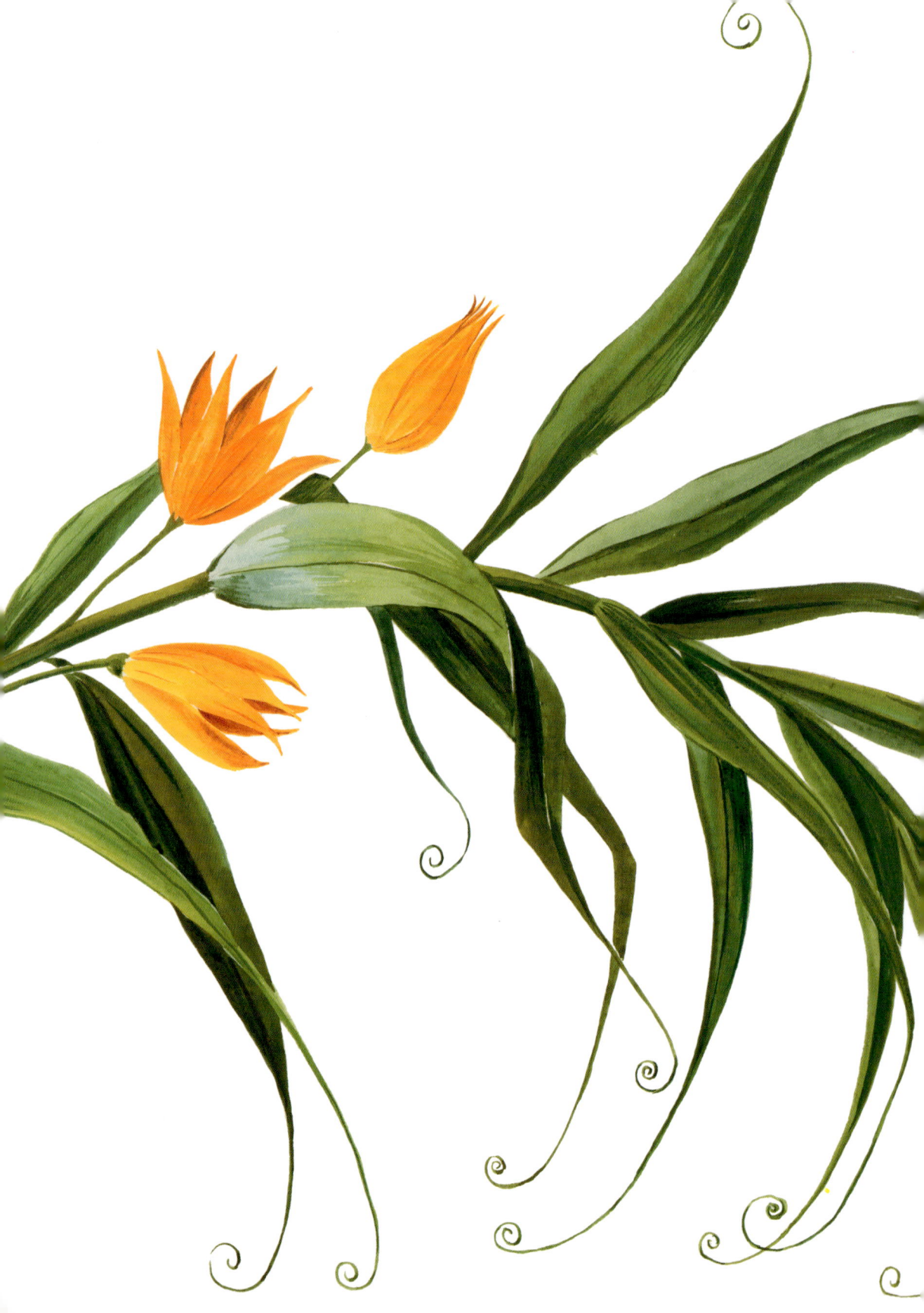

week 38

SEPTEMBER

Monday **13**

Tuesday **14**

First Quarter

Wednesday **15**

Thursday **16**

Friday **17**

Day of Atonement (Yom Kippur)

Saturday **18**

Sunday **19**

Littonia modesta. Coloured drawing by Lilian Snelling, made for H.J. Elwes of Colesbourne in August 1916.

SEPTEMBER

WEEK **39**

20 *Monday*

21 *Tuesday*

22 *Wednesday*

23 *Thursday*

Autumnal Equinox (Autumn begins)
First Day of Tabernacles (Succoth)
Full Moon

24 *Friday*

25 *Saturday*

Malvern Autumn Show (RHS)

26 *Sunday*

Malvern Autumn Show (RHS)

Nerine 'Mansellii', *Nerine flexuosa* 'Alba' × *Nerine* 'Lady St Oswald'.
coloured drawing by Lilian Snelling, made for
H.J. Elwes of Colesbourne in December 1916.

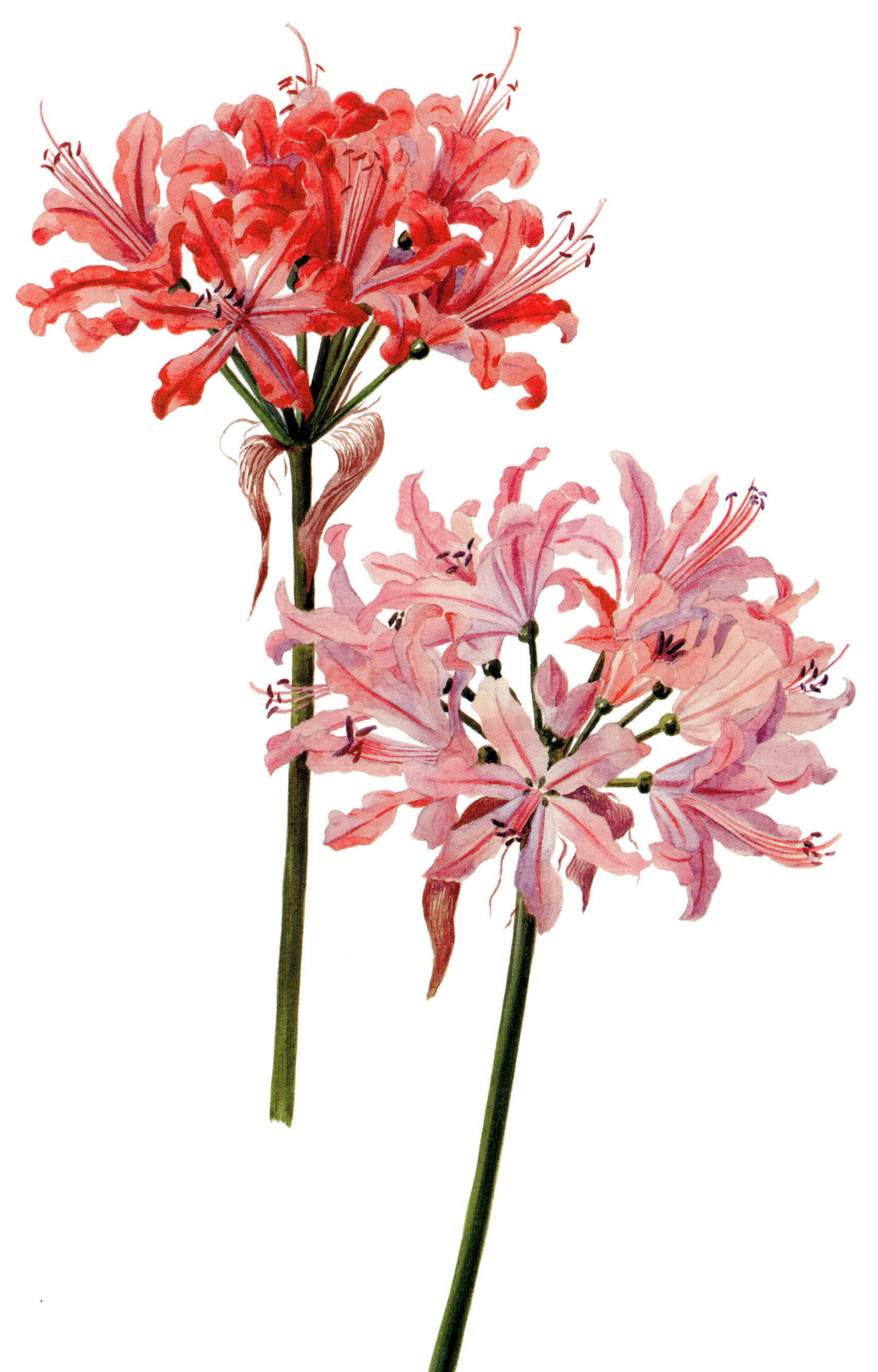

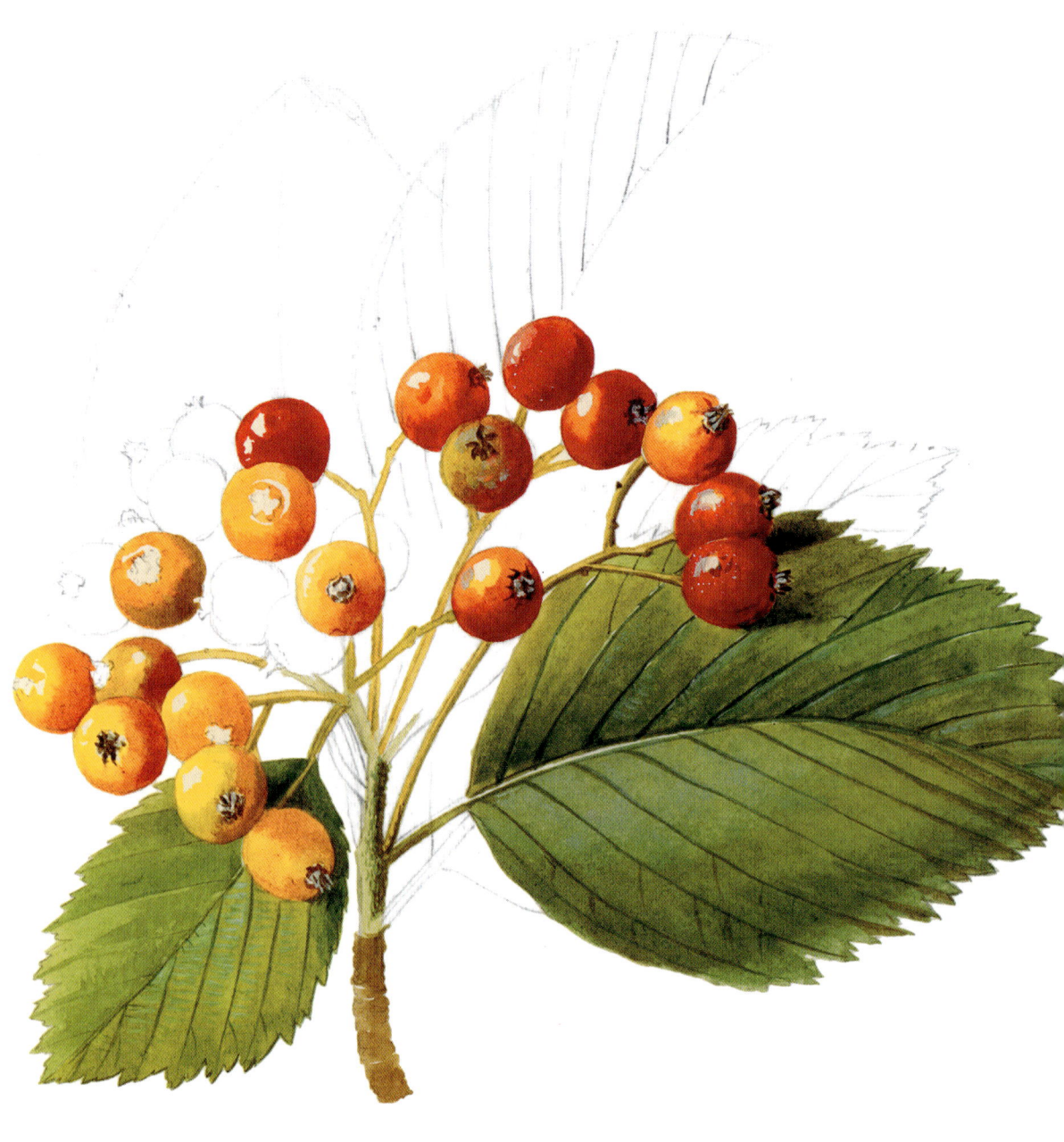

WEEK **40**

SEPTEMBER & OCTOBER

Monday **27**

Tuesday **28**

Michaelmas Day | *Wednesday* **29**

Thursday **30**

Last Quarter | *Friday* **1**

Saturday **2**

Sunday **3**

Pyrus aria [now *Sorbus aria*]. Coloured drawing, undated, by Lilian Snelling.

OCTOBER

WEEK **41**

4 *Monday* — Holiday, Australia (Labour Day)

5 *Tuesday* — RHS London Autumn Harvest Show

6 *Wednesday* — RHS London Autumn Harvest Show

7 *Thursday* — *New Moon*

8 *Friday*

9 *Saturday*

10 *Sunday*

Urceolina aurea [now *Urceolina pendula*]. Coloured drawing by Lilian Snelling, made for H.J. Elwes of Colesbourne in September 1914.

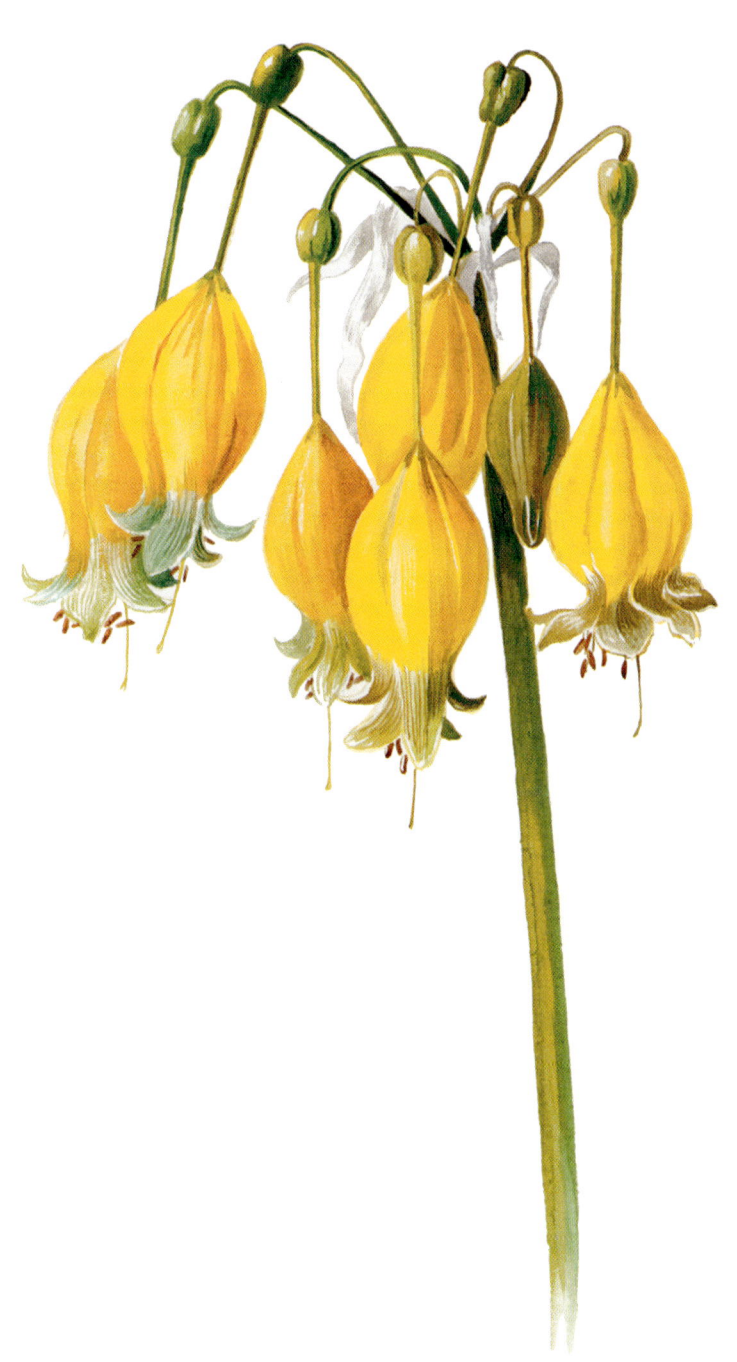

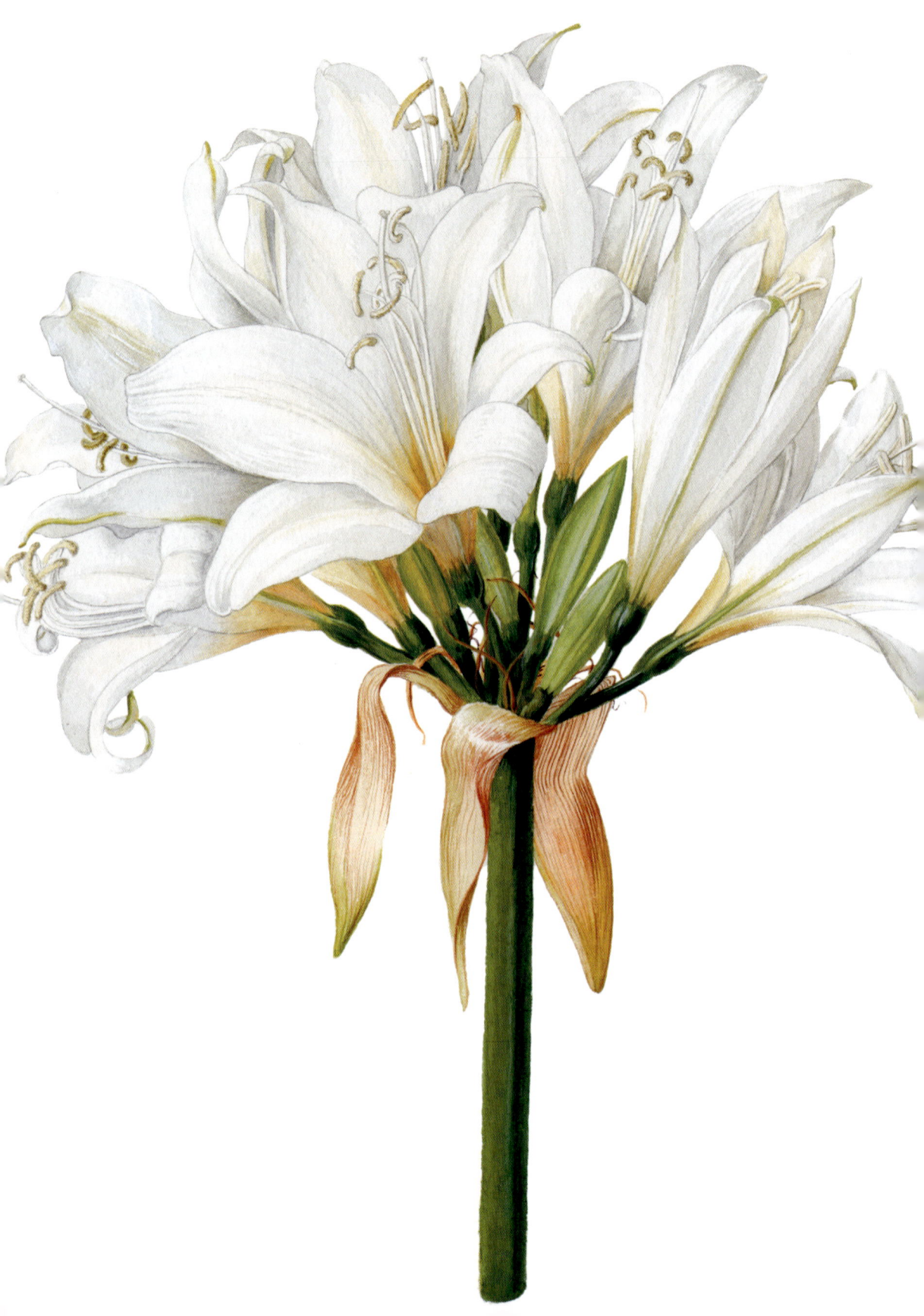

WEEK **42**

OCTOBER

Holiday, USA (Columbus Day)
Holiday, Canada (Thanksgiving)

Monday **11**

Tuesday **12**

Wednesday **13**

First Quarter

Thursday **14**

Friday **15**

Saturday **16**

Sunday **17**

Amaryllis belladonna 'Hathor'. Coloured drawing, undated, by Lilian Snelling, for a plate published in the *Journal of the Royal Horticultural Society* in 1951, to accompany an article by Hugh Farmar about *Amaryllis belladonna* and its cultivars.

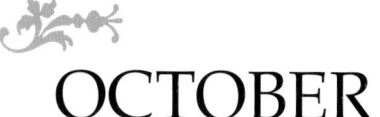

OCTOBER

WEEK **43**

18 *Monday*

19 *Tuesday*

20 *Wednesday*

21 *Thursday*

22 *Friday*

23 *Saturday* — Full Moon

24 *Sunday* — United Nations Day

Top: *Rubus fruticosus*. Coloured drawing, undated.
Bottom: *Viburnum opulus*. Coloured drawing, undated.
Both by Lilian Snelling.

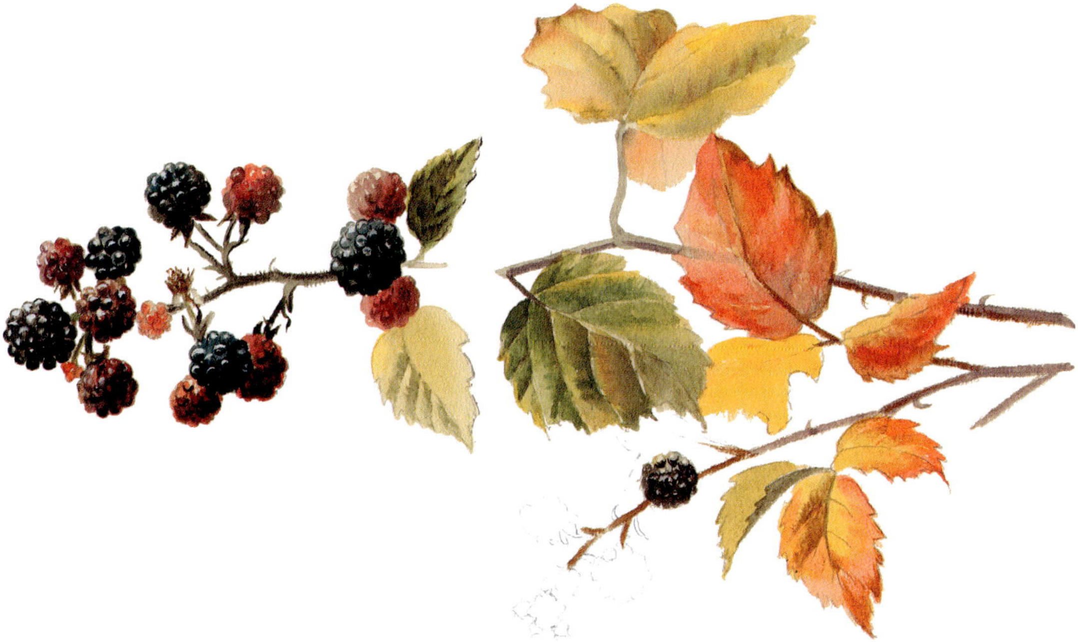

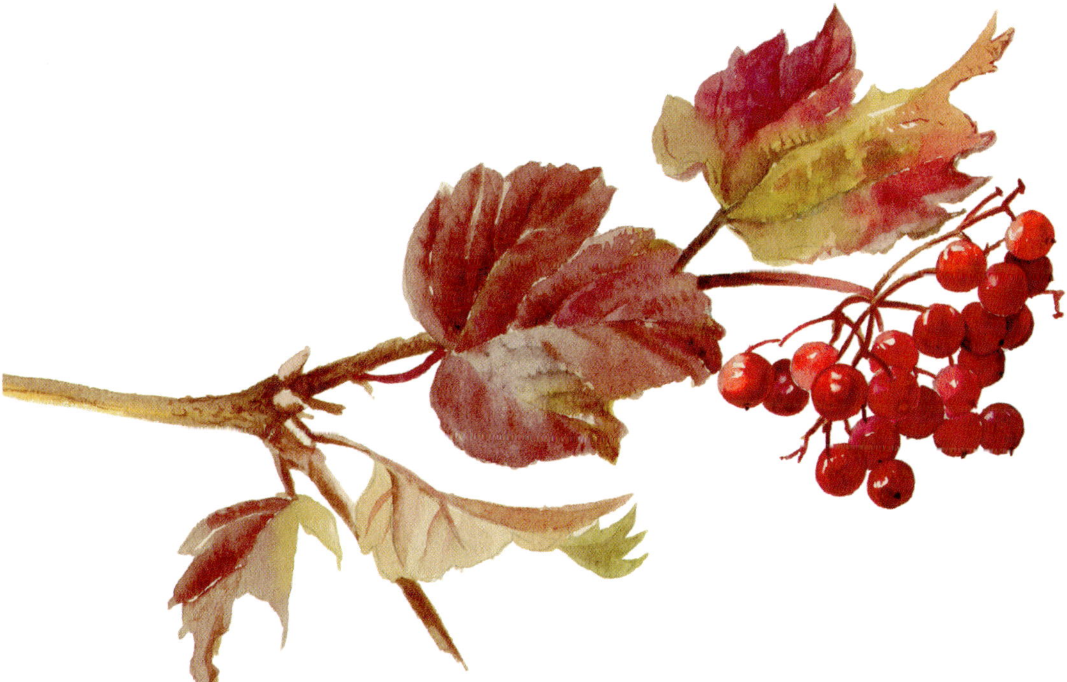

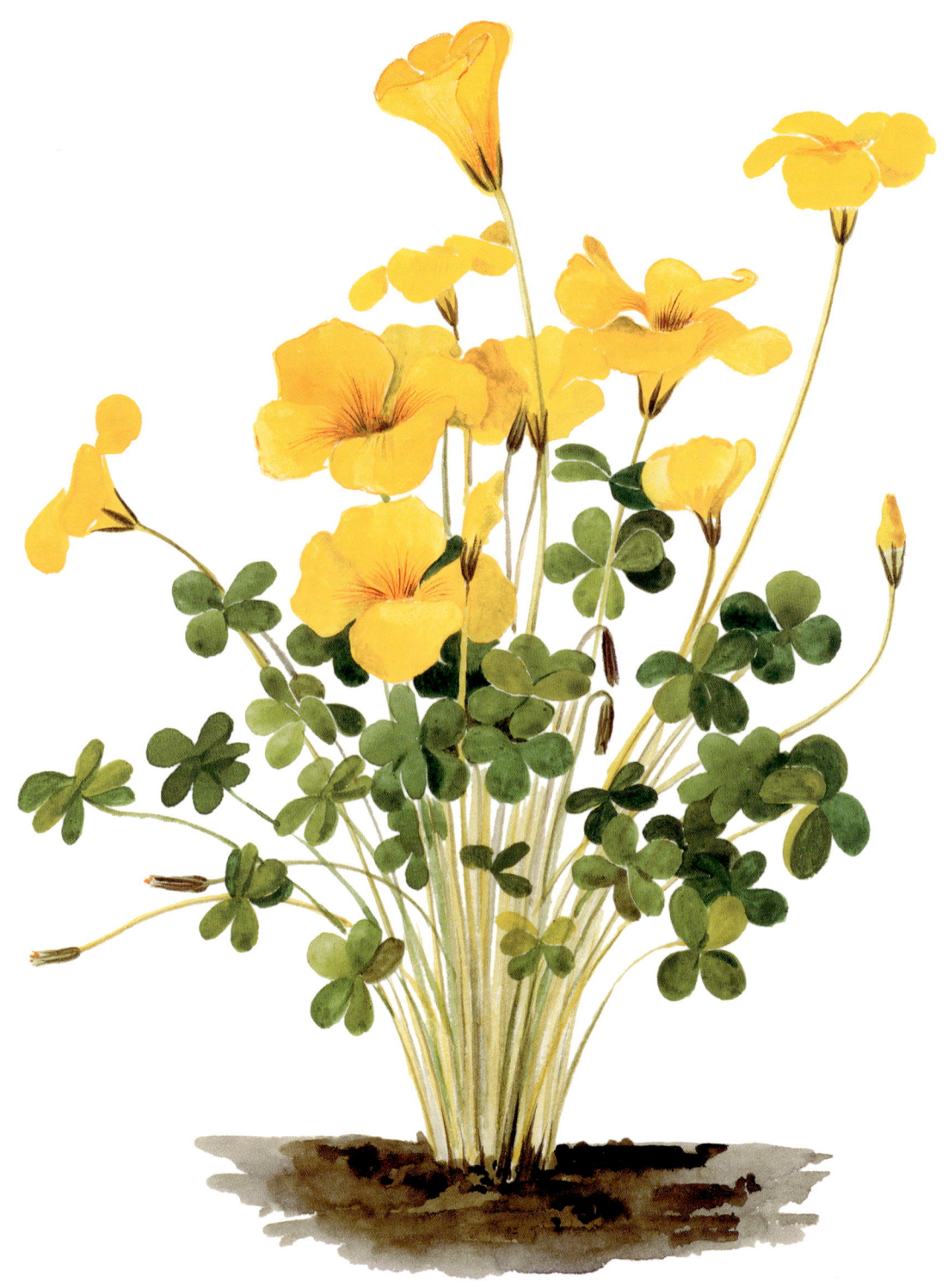

WEEK **44**

OCTOBER

Holiday, Republic of Ireland
Holiday, New Zealand (Labour Day)

Monday **25**

Tuesday **26**

Wednesday **27**

Thursday **28**

Friday **29**

Last Quarter

Saturday **30**

British Summer Time ends
Hallowe'en

Sunday **31**

Oxalis lobata [now *Oxalis perdicaria*]. Coloured drawing by Lilian Snelling, made for H.J. Elwes of Colesbourne in September 1915.

NOVEMBER

WEEK **45**

1 *Monday* All Saints' Day

2 *Tuesday*

3 *Wednesday*

4 *Thursday*

5 *Friday* Guy Fawkes' Day

6 *Saturday* *New Moon*

7 *Sunday*

Dipsacus pilosus. Coloured drawing, dated August 1933, by Lilian Snelling, based on a specimen found in Somerset.

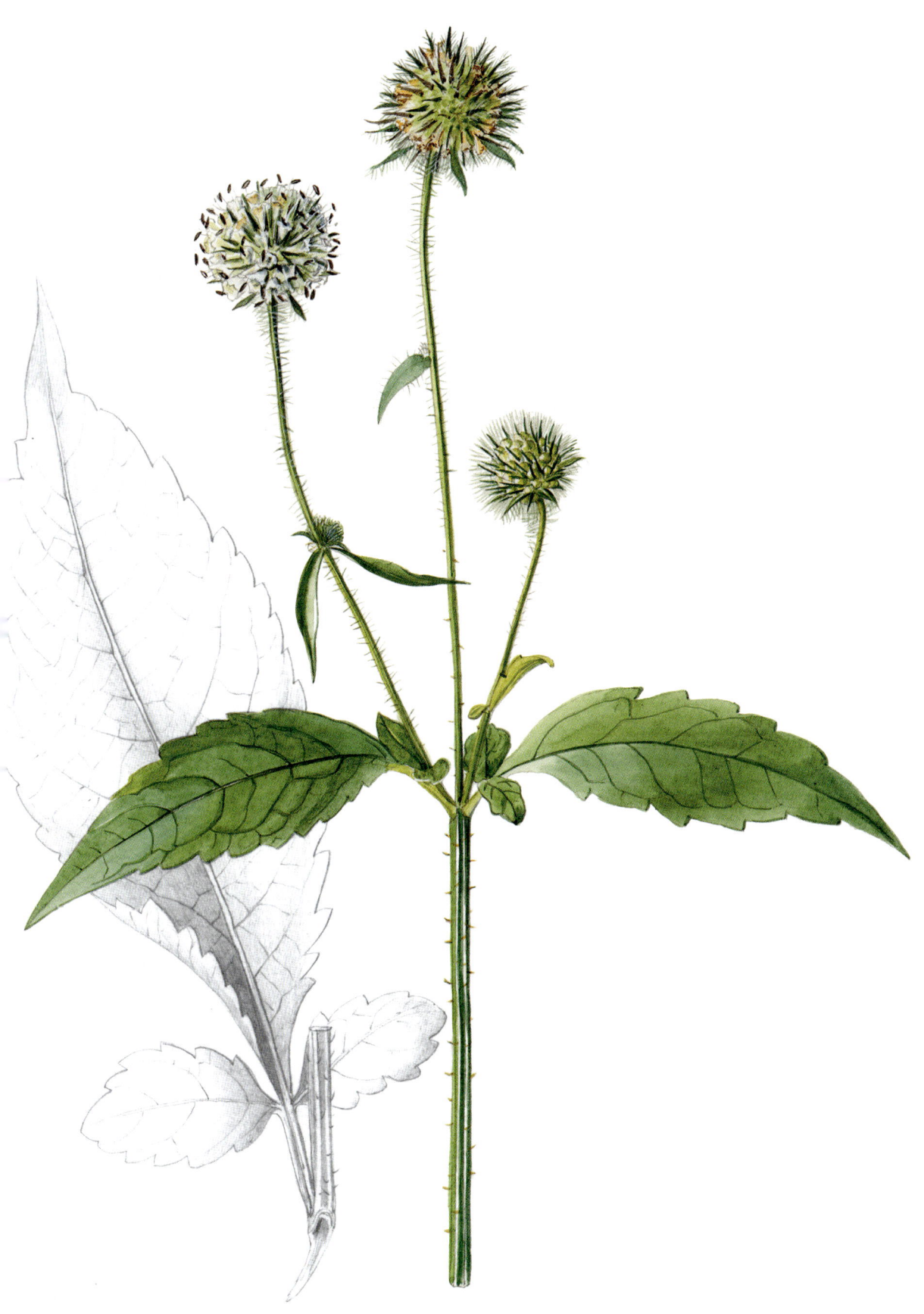

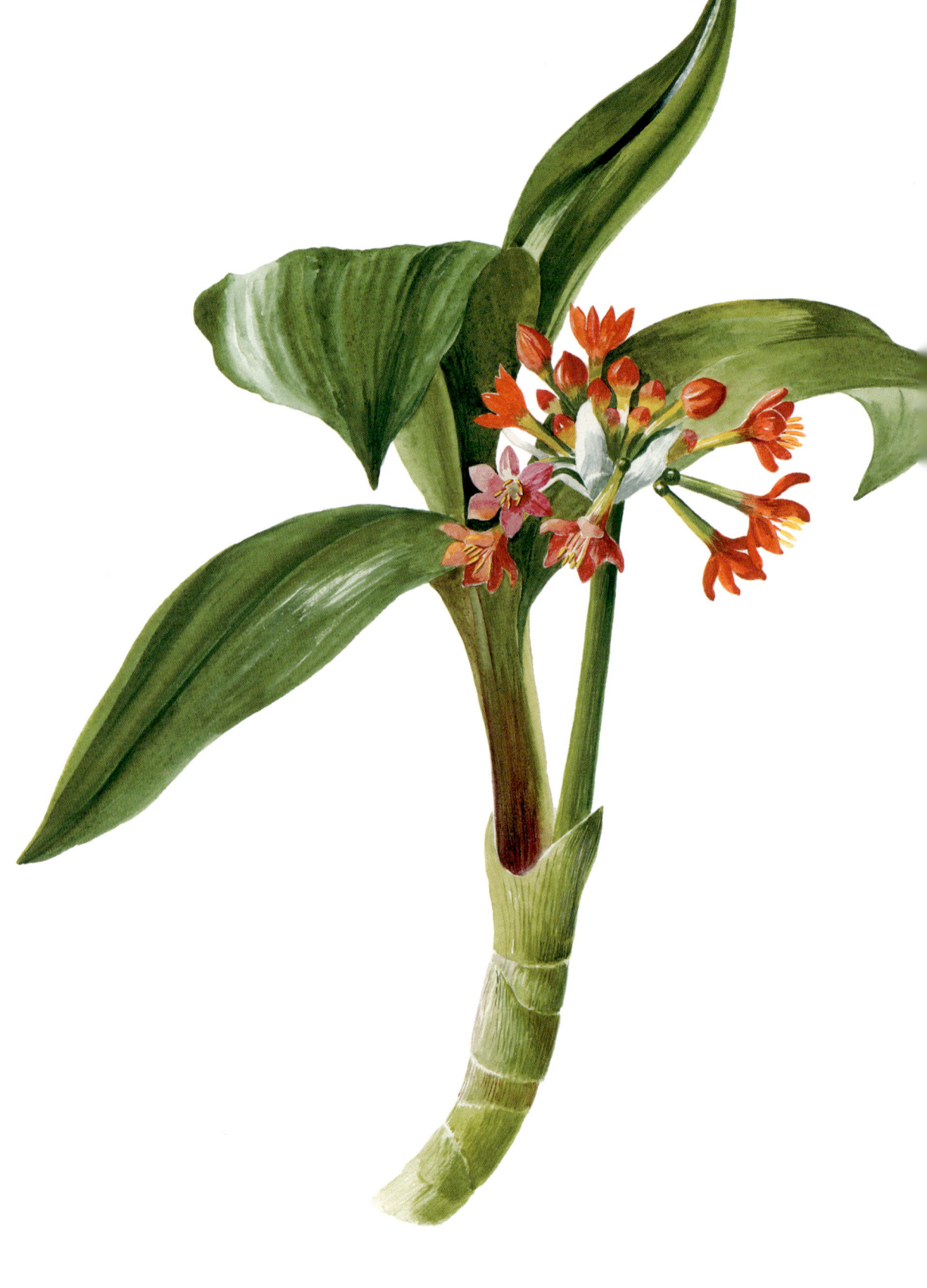

WEEK **46**

NOVEMBER

Monday **8**

Tuesday **9**

Wednesday **10**

Holiday, USA (Veterans Day)
Holiday, Canada (Remembrance Day)

Thursday **11**

Friday **12**

First Quarter

Saturday **13**

Remembrance Sunday, UK

Sunday **14**

Choananthus cyrtanthiflorus [now *Haemanthus cyrtanthiflorus*]. Coloured drawing by Lilian Snelling, made for H.J. Elwes of Colesbourne in August 1915. It bears a label stating that W.B. Turrill, the future Keeper of the Kew Herbarium but then still a young assistant, determined the name.

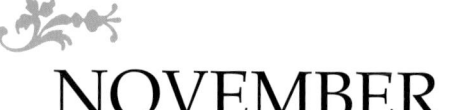

NOVEMBER

WEEK **47**

15 *Monday*

16 *Tuesday*

17 *Wednesday*

18 *Thursday*

19 *Friday*

20 *Saturday*

21 *Sunday* *Full Moon*

Schisandra sphenanthera.
Hand-coloured proof plate by Lilian Snelling, for
plate 8921 of *Curtis's Botanical Magazine* (1938).

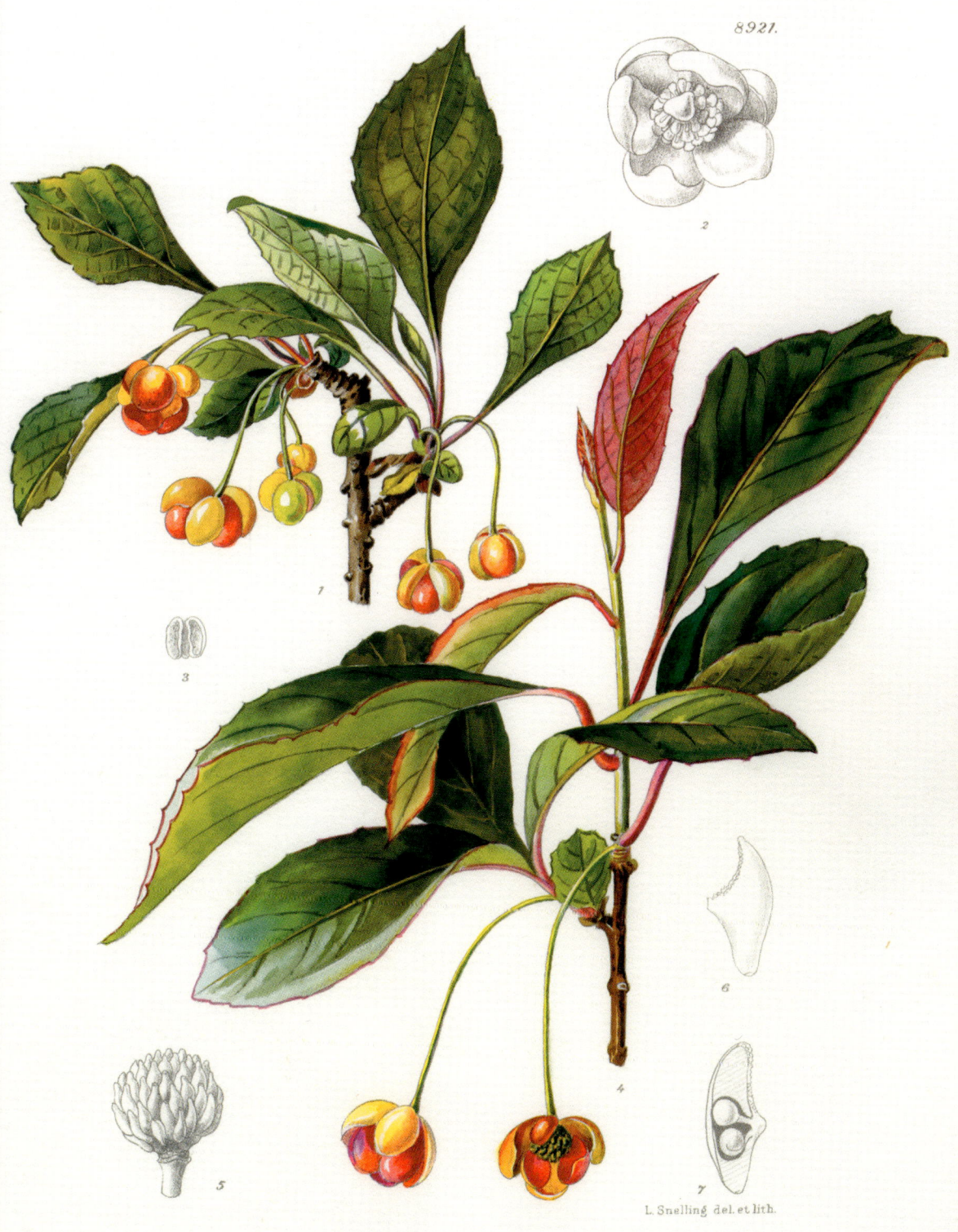

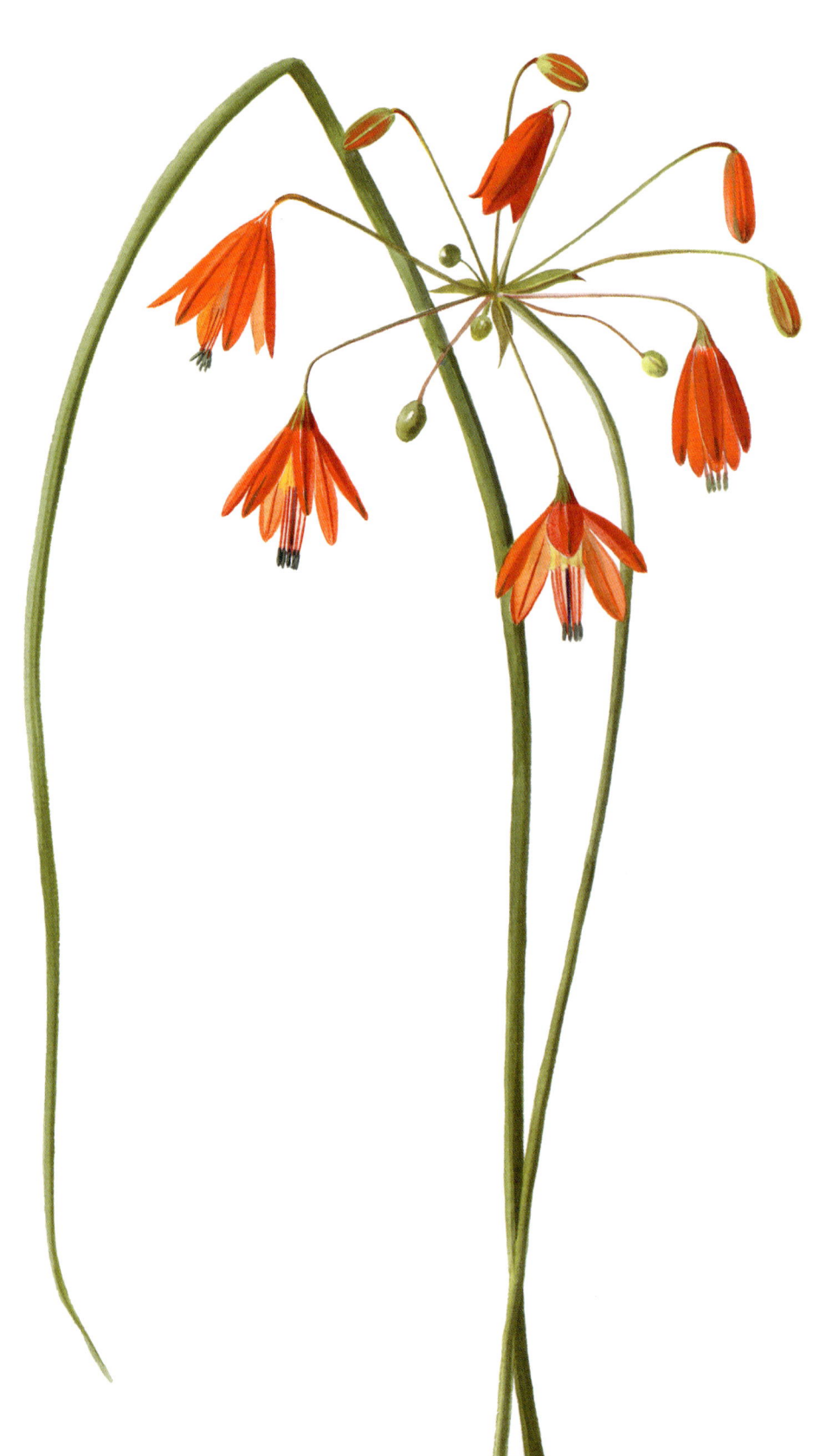

WEEK **48**

NOVEMBER

Monday **22**

Tuesday **23**

Wednesday **24**

Holiday, USA (Thanksgiving Day)

Thursday **25**

Friday **26**

Saturday **27**

First Sunday in Advent
Last Quarter

Sunday **28**

Bessera elegans. Coloured drawing by Lilian Snelling, made for H.J. Elwes of Colesbourne in October 1915.

NOVEMBER & DECEMBER

WEEK **49**

29 *Monday*

30 *Tuesday*   St. Andrew's Day

1 *Wednesday*

2 *Thursday*   Jewish Festival of Chanukah, First Day

3 *Friday*

4 *Saturday*

5 *Sunday*   *New Moon*

Bromelia sp. Coloured drawing, undated, by Lilian Snelling.

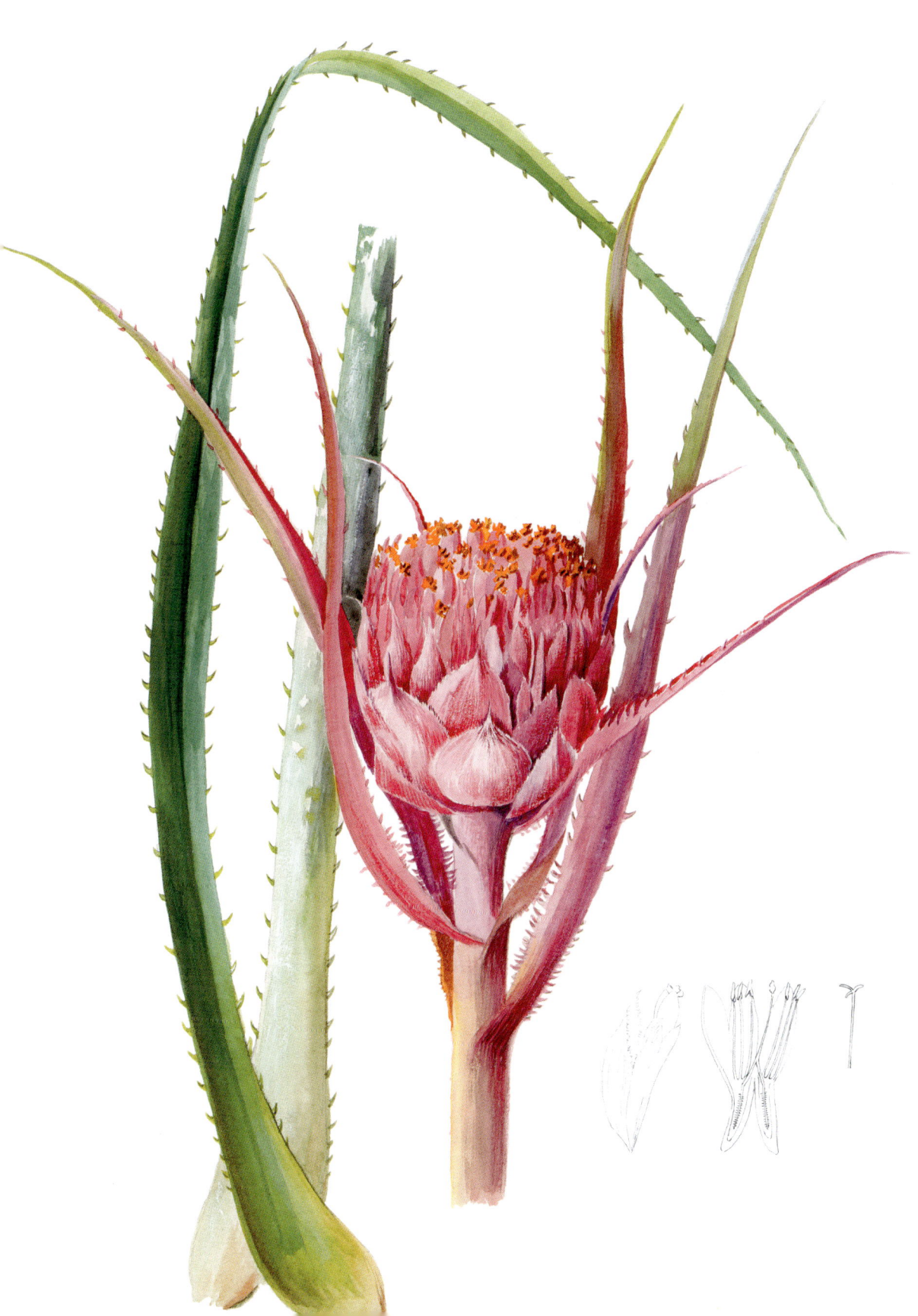

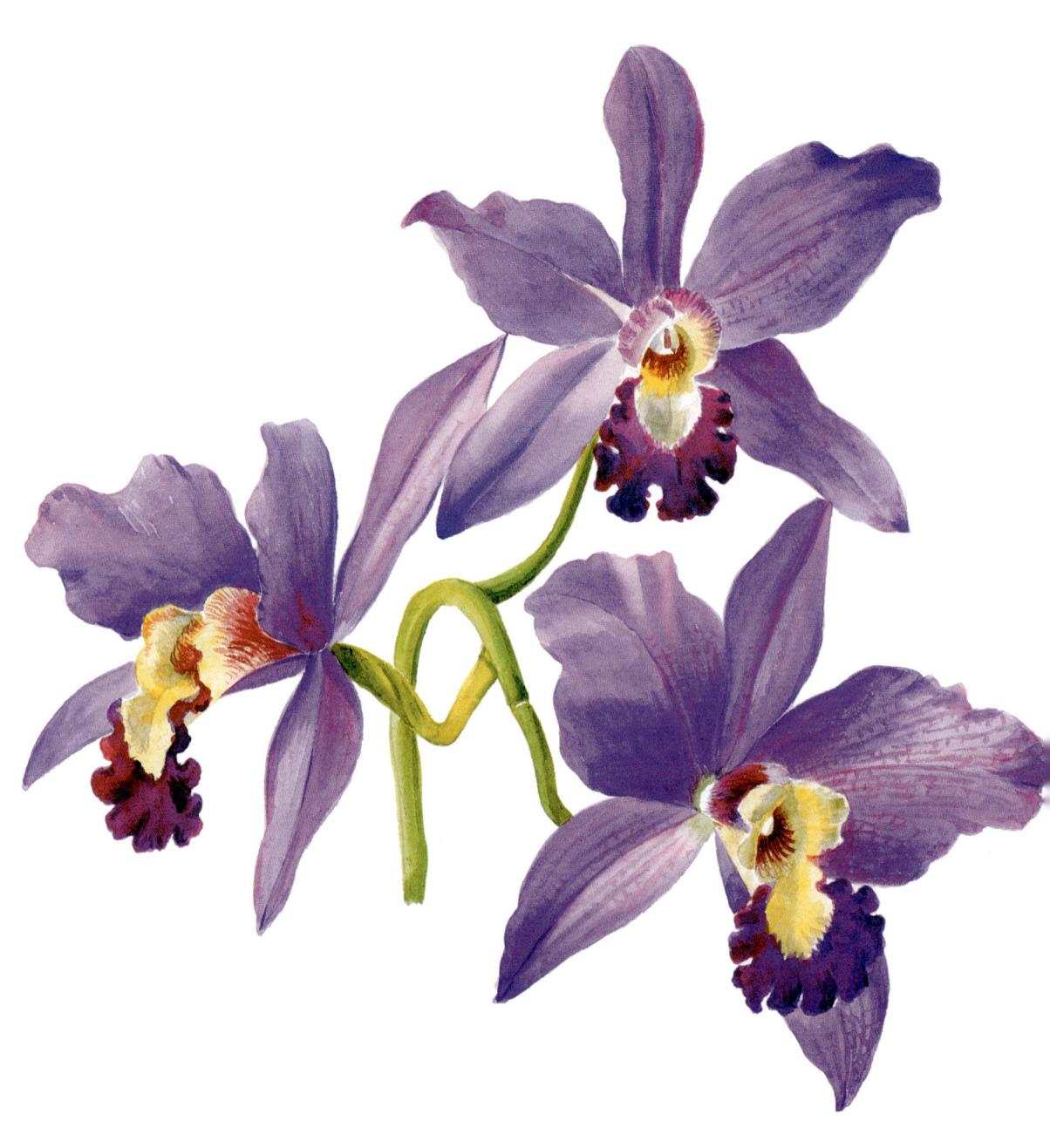

WEEK **50**

DECEMBER

Monday **6**

Tuesday **7**

Islamic New Year (subject to sighting of the moon)

Wednesday **8**

Thursday **9**

Friday **10**

Saturday **11**

Sunday **12**

Cymbidium sp. Coloured drawing, undated, by Lilian Snelling.

DECEMBER

WEEK **51**

13 *Monday* — *First Quarter*

14 *Tuesday*

15 *Wednesday*

16 *Thursday*

17 *Friday*

18 *Saturday*

19 *Sunday*

Calceolaria 'John Innes'. Coloured drawing by Lilian Snelling, made for H.J. Elwes of Colesbourne in July 1916.

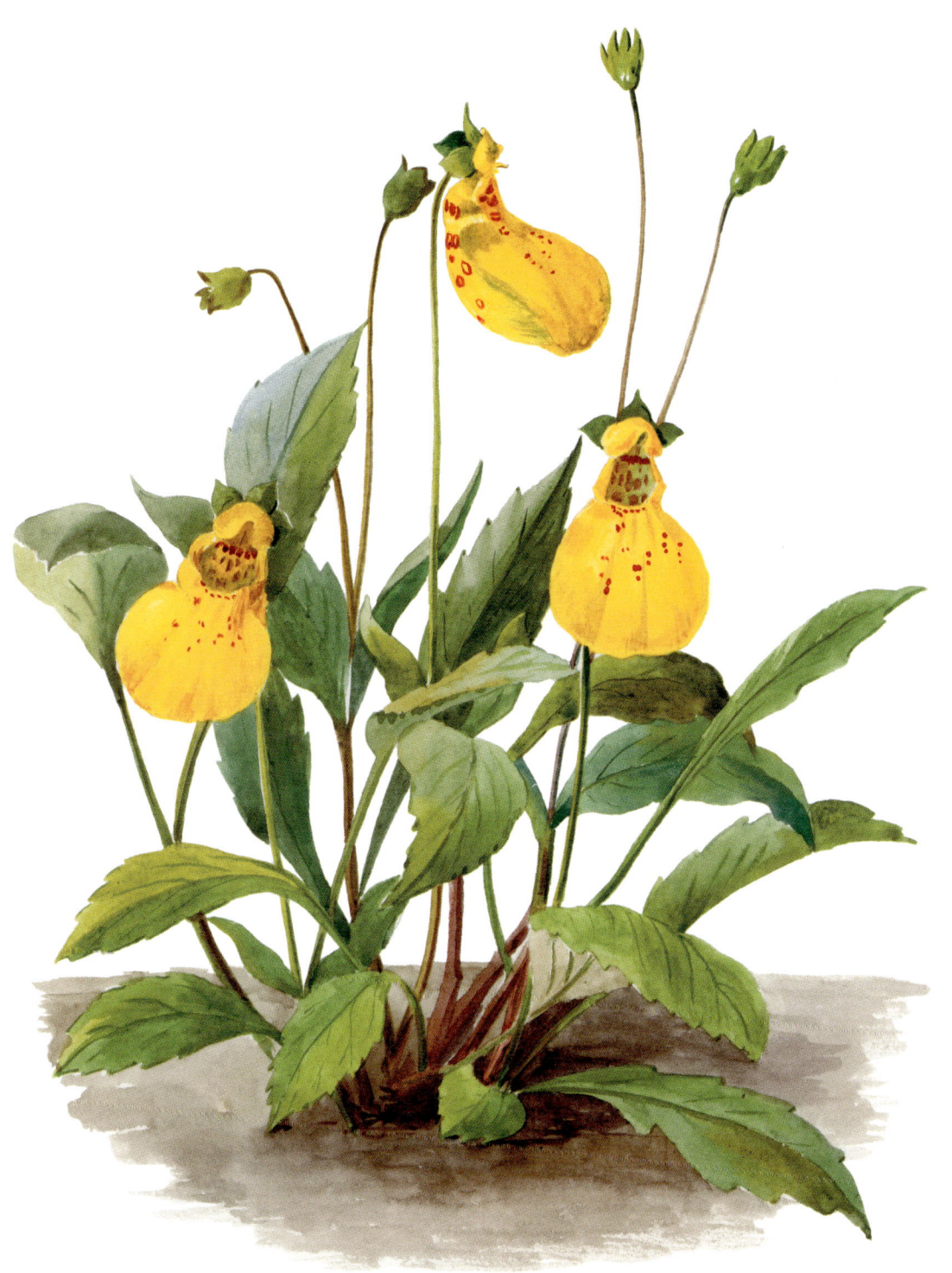

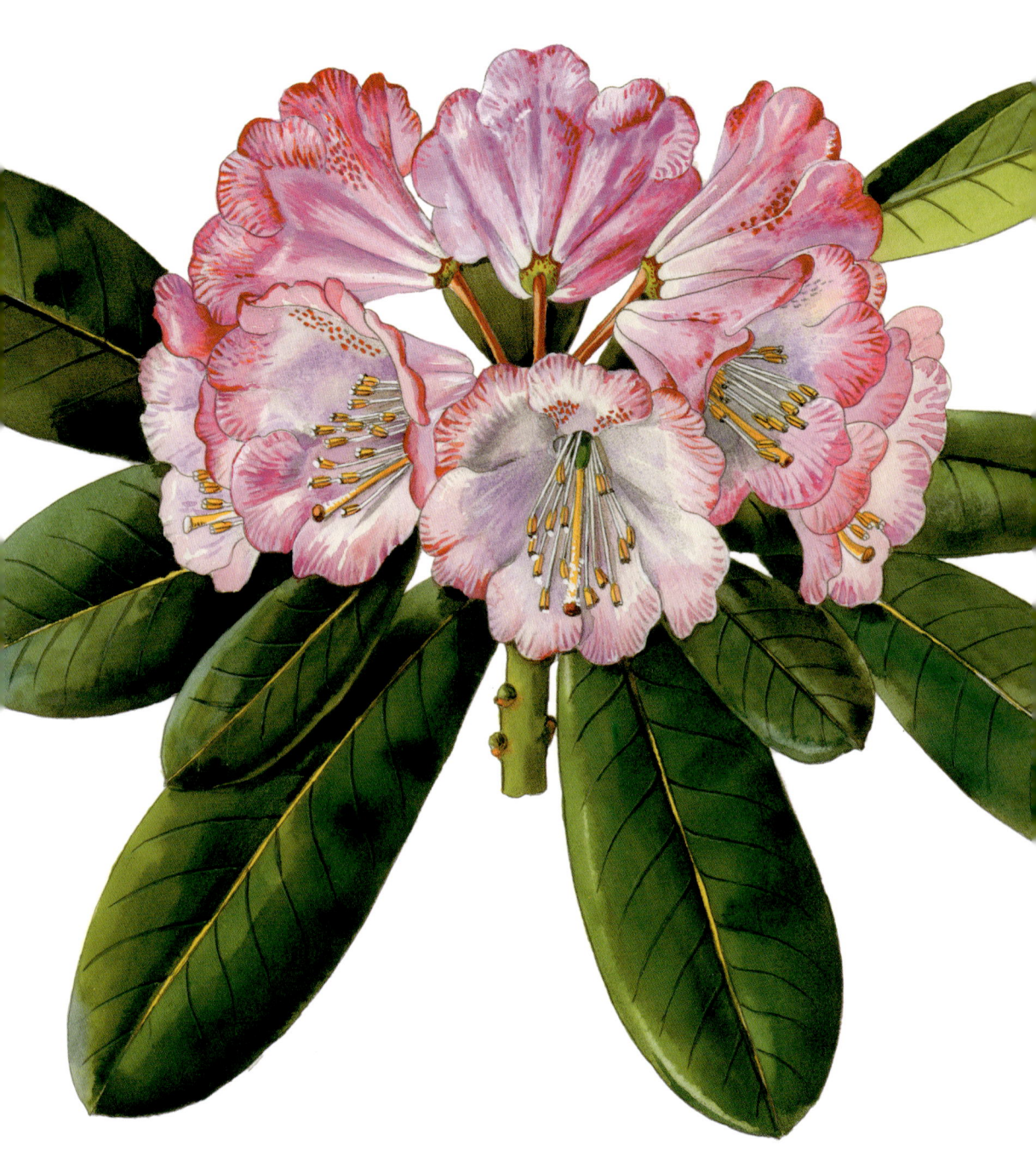

WEEK **52**

DECEMBER

Monday **20**

Tuesday **21**

Winter Solstice (Winter begins)
Full Moon

Wednesday **22**

Thursday **23**

Christmas Eve
Holiday, USA

Friday **24**

Christmas Day
Holiday, UK, Republic of Ireland and Canada

Saturday **25**

Boxing Day (St. Stephen's Day)

Sunday **26**

Rhododendron vernicosum. Hand-coloured proof plate by Lilian
Snelling, for plate 8904–5 of *Curtis's Botanical Magazine* (1938).

DECEMBER & JANUARY

WEEK 53

27 *Monday*

28 *Tuesday*

Holiday, UK and New Zealand
Last Quarter

29 *Wednesday*

30 *Thursday*

31 *Friday*

New Year's Eve
Holiday, USA

1 *Saturday*

New Year's Day

2 *Sunday*

Erica vagans. Coloured drawing, dated August 1936, by Lilian Snelling, based on a specimen found at Coverack in Cornwall.

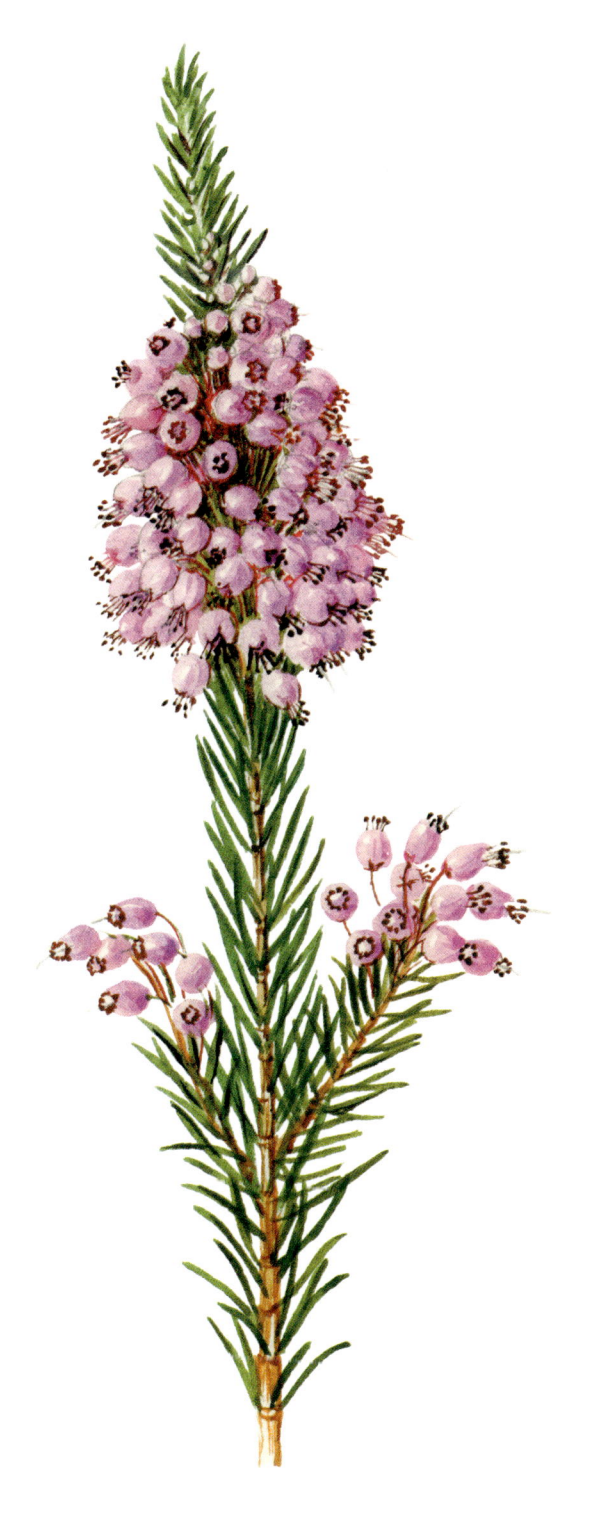

EUROPEAN NATIONAL HOLIDAYS 2010

AUSTRIA	Jan 1, 6; Apr 5; May 1, 23; Jun 3; Aug 15; Oct 26; Nov 1; Dec 8, 25, 26
BELGIUM	Jan 1; Apr 2, 4, 5; May 1, 13, 23, 24; Jul 21; Aug 15; Nov 1, 11; Dec 25
BULGARIA	Jan 1; Mar 3; Apr 5; May 1, 6, 24; Sep 6, 22; Dec 24, 25, 26
CROATIA	Jan 1, 6; Apr 4, 5; May 1; Jun 3, 22, 25; Aug 5, 15; Oct 8; Nov 1; Dec 25, 26
CYPRUS	Jan 1; Mar 25; Apr 1, 2, 4, 5; May 1; Aug 15; Oct 1; Dec 25, 26
CZECH REPUBLIC	Jan 1; Apr 5; May 1, 8; Jul 5, 6; Sep 28; Oct 28; Nov 17; Dec 24, 25, 26
DENMARK	Jan 1; Apr 1, 2, 5; May 1, 23; Jun 5; Dec 25, 26
ESTONIA	Jan 1; Feb 24; Apr 2, 4; May 1, 23; Jun 5; Dec 24, 25, 26
FINLAND	Jan 1, 6; Apr 2, 4, 5; May 1, 13, 23; Nov 6; Dec 6, 25, 26
FRANCE	Jan 1; Apr 4; May 1, 8, 23; Jul 14; Aug 15; Nov 1, 11; Dec 25
GERMANY	Jan 1; Apr 2, 5; May 1, 13, 24; Oct 3; Dec 25, 26
GREECE	Jan 1, 6; Mar 25; Apr 2, 5; May 1; Aug 15; Oct 28; Dec 25, 26
HUNGARY	Jan 1; Mar 15; Apr 5; May 1, 23; Aug 20; Oct 23; Nov 1; Dec 25, 26
ITALY	Jan 1, 6; Apr 5, 25; May 1; Jun 2; Aug 15; Nov 1; Dec 8, 25, 26
LATVIA	Jan 1; Apr 2, 4, 5; May 1, 4; Jun 23, 24; Nov 18; Dec 25, 26, 31
LITHUANIA	Jan 1; Feb 16; Mar 11; Apr 5; May 1, 2; Jun 24; Jul 6; Aug 15; Nov 1; Dec 25, 26, 28
LUXEMBOURG	Jan 1; Feb 19; Apr 5; May 1, 13, 23; Jun 23; Aug 15; Nov 1; Dec 25, 26
MALTA	Jan 1; Feb 10; Mar 19, 31; Apr 2; May 1; Jun 7, 29; Aug 15; Sep 8, 21; Dec 8, 13, 25
NETHERLANDS	Jan 1; Apr 2, 4, 5, 30; May 4, 5, 13, 23; Dec 23, 25, 26
NORWAY	Jan 1; Mar 28, Apr 1, 2, 4, 5; May 1, 17, 13, 23, 24; Dec 25, 26
POLAND	Jan 1; Apr 4, 5; May 1, 3, 23; Jun 3; Aug 15; Oct 5, Nov 1, 11; Dec 25, 26
PORTUGAL	Jan 1; Apr 2, 4, 25; May 1; Jun 3, 10; Aug 15; Oct 5, Nov 1; Dec 1, 8, 25
ROMANIA	Jan 1, 2; Apr 4, 5; May 1; Dec 1, 25, 26
SLOVAKIA	Jan 1, 6; Apr 2, 5; May 1, 8; Jul 5; Aug 29; Sep 1, 15, Nov 1, 17; Dec 24, 25, 26
SLOVENIA	Jan 1, 2; Feb 8; Apr 4, 5, 27; May 1, 2; Jun 25; Aug 15; Oct 31; Nov 1; Dec 25, 26
SPAIN	Jan 1; Apr 2; May 1; Aug 15; Oct 12; Nov 1; Dec 6, 8, 25
SWEDEN	Jan 1, 6; Apr 2, 4 ,5; May 1, 13, 23; Jun 6, 26; Nov 6; Dec 25, 26
SWITZERLAND	Jan 1, 2; Apr 2, 5, 13, 24; May 1, 21, 31; Aug 1; Dec 25, 26